Small Handprints on My Classroom Door; Small Handprints on My Heart

Small Handprints on My Classroom Door; Small Handprints on My Heart

Early Childhood Teaching Standards in Practice

Robin Johns and Rocky Wallace

ROWMAN & LITTLEFIELD
Lanham • Boulder • New York • London

Published by Rowman & Littlefield
A wholly owned subsidiary of The Rowman & Littlefield Publishing Group, Inc.
4501 Forbes Boulevard, Suite 200, Lanham, Maryland 20706
www.rowman.com

Unit A, Whitacre Mews, 26-34 Stannary Street, London SE11 4AB

British Library Cataloguing in Publication Information Available

Library of Congress Cataloging-in-Publication Data

Johns, Robin.
Small handprints on my classroom door; small handprints on my heart : early childhood teaching standards in practice / Robin Johns and Rocky Wallace.
pages cm
Includes bibliographical references.
ISBN 978-1-4758-1823-9 (cloth : alk. paper) — ISBN 978-1-4758-1824-6 (pbk. : alk. paper) — ISBN 978-1-4758-1825-3 (electronic)
1. Early childhood education—Curricula--United States. 2. Early childhood education—Standards—United States. 3. Curriculum planning—United States. I. Title.
LB1139.4.J64 2015
372.21—dc23
2015006763

Printed in the United States of America

We dedicate this book to our parents, who taught us about the importance of faith, family, honorable work, and lifetime learning. Mom and Dad felt a call on their lives to be great parents. They were, and they still are.

Contents

Foreword ix

Preface xi

Acknowledgments xiii

1   Early Intervention 1

2   Cinderella 7

3   The Wheels on the Bus 15

4   Poster Child 23

5   Moonlighting 31

6   Miss Teacher: (If This Toddler Could Talk) 41

7   Mrs. Carwall's Student 47

8   Ratios 55

9   Stella Rae 63

10 Boy Interrupted 71

11 Lament of a Working Mother 79

12 They Have Parents 85

13 Come August 93

14 Educating the Masses 99

15 Closing Thoughts 107

References 111

About the Authors 113

Foreword

For a real dose of reality intended especially for today's early childhood classrooms, *Small Handprints On My Classroom Door; Small Handprints on My Heart: Early Childhood Teaching Standards in Practice* will register with anyone who is involved with early childhood and elementary school settings. Each chapter's schoolhouse story is tied to an NAEYC standard. The principal and teachers tell their very personal narratives which are applicable to any early childhood program. Then at the end of each chapter a "Reflections" section, followed by a "Solutions" section, provides both stimulating and insightful questions, accompanied by potential resolutions which are supported by research-based references.

Ultimately, this book provides a thorough and comprehensive look into today's early childhood classrooms: the joys and challenges that are so authentic, the staff who dutifully attends to their work, and the students who benefit from these efforts!

It will resonate especially with early childhood advocates both far and wide.

Mike Armstrong, Executive Director
Kentucky School Boards Association

Preface

As a brother and sister team who have been educators our entire careers and who have enjoyed writing since we were children, this has been a labor of love. In the following pages, we simply dissect the interesting, inspiring, and sometimes lonely world of the early childhood teacher. We share insights that a caring principal might have if he or she understands on a deep level the complex world of being a teacher of young children.

As the continued across the board advancements in education hint at a brighter future for our children and our society, we are troubled that some of the same practices that have prevented earlier generations of students and teachers from prospering in the classroom are still commonplace.

Our hope is that this book will touch the hearts of teachers, administrators, and parents who know deep down that we still have such a long way to go, and who understand that the tasks we assign our teachers are sometimes overwhelming.

A great classroom will have a teacher who cares deeply for the children entrusted to his or her care. A great school will continually forge ahead in providing the necessary human resources, tools, training, and support in the affective domain that teachers so desperately need in order to have meaningful, fulfilling careers that impact every student positively in profound ways. . . . Enjoy.

Rocky Wallace and Robin Johns

Acknowledgments

We would not be able to begin to weave these stories, which mirror the real work of teachers and principals who are down in the trenches, if not for the children and youth who we have been blessed to work with, and our colleagues.

To all of those students who have so enriched our lives, and to those faithful souls who lead by tirelessly serving in the classroom day after day, we say thank you.

To the college students of education who have a heart for children and bring fresh ideas to the early childhood classroom, we say thank you.

And, we are forever grateful to Dr. Tom Koerner and his dedicated and talented team at Rowman & Littlefield. Dr. Koerner continues to believe in the heart and the voice of the school leader who is in the trenches.

ONE

Early Intervention

NAEYC STANDARD 4: USING DEVELOPMENTALLY EFFECTIVE
APPROACHES TO CONNECT WITH CHILDREN AND FAMILIES

*2b: Supporting and Engaging Families and Communities through Respectful,
Reciprocal Relationships*

Someday, she should write a book. It would be in the flavor of the
James Herriot series—those fascinating folktales of a veterinarian in the
mountains. His was named *All Creatures Great and Small.*

Hers would be *Tiny People, Tall Services.* It would have to be anonymous, and she would have to disguise her students and their families.
But somehow, she would still convey how inevitably they gripped your
heart.

How it felt to hear, as you tapped lightly on the door, the pitter-patter
of little feet, and your name sung out by a small voice—"Camine," "Ja
Ja," or whatever version of "Jasmine" they could articulate. Or if the big
door was open, there were the Dennis the Menace twins standing in the
storm door grinning at you sheepishly, their enormous eyes and deep
dimples beckoning you to come in.

Let in the door by tots—this was an honor one could never deserve,
no matter how many hours you spent collecting toys and tricks, no matter how many websites you searched late at night, no matter how far out
to the end of nowhere you traveled. Never, never could a peddler have
had a grander entrance than at the doorway of a toddler's heart.

"Hi, Dennis. Hi, Dalton. We have so much to do! Did you help Daddy this week?" With all the self-restraint she could muster, she resisted the urge to pinch their chubby, little arms and legs. Never in her life had she imagined that patrons could be so absolutely irresistible as was with this caseload. But she had suspected all along that she would fall in love with her young students.

It was the families that took her heart by surprise.

How would she ever be able to convey, in her book, how it felt to be a guest in their homes, how her heart would swell with pride when she heard a parent say to an acquaintance on the phone, "Audrey's therapist is here"?

She knew from experience how stressful it was to have company on a weekly basis, and she tried her best to put their minds at rest when they apologized for the house.

Some of the mothers were experienced, adding to her nervousness at trying to engage an eighteen-month-old for an hour in the presence of his family.

Others were young and struggling. She wanted to mother them as much as she did the children, to deliver them from the temptations lingering outside their door.

And at least half of them were making it on meager means. She would notice the modest conditions around her and suddenly feel ashamed of her iPhone 6 and her touch-screen laptop. Once, she changed from her boots to her shoes in the car so not to flaunt her affluence.

Though teaching tots and infants with their families present never became completely comfortable for her, she did learn to embrace the opportunity to teach the families as well. She modeled turning small things into learning experiences, seizing the opportunity to incorporate nursery rhymes and social play into daily activities.

There were moments (that were not in her lesson plans) of bonding with the families: spontaneous laughter; sharing recipes and regrets.

Sometimes the toddler's needs were profound. She didn't know how anything could be more poignant than when the mother would follow her out to the car after her first intervention with her child and ask, "So, what do you think?"

She had not expected to be the parents' lifeline to hope. It was a scary role to play. But their trust motivated her to work that much harder researching and trying new ideas. Then, sometimes after many weeks, there would be a breakthrough—the toddler would suddenly perform the task they had all worked so hard on. A spontaneous celebration would ensue: a cry of victory and a round of applause from the mother, the tot, and herself.

How would she ever convey in her book the different personalities, the moments of joy? Once, in the farmhouse of Elmer and Opal, an elderly couple who babysat one of her tots (Caleb), a children's picture book of songs turned up in the toy box.

It had been a wonderful lesson. Caleb's two siblings were home from school that day for snow, and Jasmine, as always, invited them to join in, as the added interaction always enriched the lesson.

The picture book had old, classical sing-alongs, including the chorus of "Skip to My Lou." She sang the knee-slapping song with her young charge and his siblings while they looked at the pictures and moved to the rhythm. But she soon ran out of verses.

That was when Elmer chimed in, "Fly's in the buttermilk, shoo, fly, shoo."

"Yeah, that's it!" rejoiced Opal.

Caleb carried his book across the room and curled up in Elmer's lap in the old easy chair. Together, the six of them sang while the logs crackled in the fireplace, and the rooster crowed out back. "Fly's in the buttermilk, shoo, fly, shoo, fly's in the buttermilk, shoo, fly, shoo . . ."

She looked around at the smiling faces—her Caleb's eyes bright as he nestled in Elmer's arms, his siblings joining in, Opal slapping her knee, and Elmer's ruddy cheeks glowing in the firelight. "Fly's in the buttermilk, shoo fly, shoo. Skip to my lou, my darlin'."

(Some pictures stay engraved in your memory forever.)

"This is joy," she thought.

She had always known she would fall in love with the children. But the families . . . and the babysitters . . . they caught her heart by surprise.

THROUGH HIS EYES

There was something about the kinship between the families and their First Steps interventionists which always got Mr. Pearson's attention. As the principal of Wesley Elementary School, he had chaired hundreds of Admissions & Release Committee (ARC) meetings, in which the parents and the child's teachers met to discuss their child's special needs and to set goals for his or her education. When a three-year-old qualified for preschool, his or her developmental interventionist or speech, occupational, or physical therapist would often attend the ARC meeting to coach the parent and advise the school.

Today, they met the famous Amos twins, and as the boys engaged in their own twin language, explored the meeting room, chased each other around the table, and participated in a little wrestling which climaxed in swatting and biting, Mr. Pearson gave the preschool teacher, Mrs. Carwall, a sympathetic glance.

Mrs. Carwall strategically invited the boys to build a castle with her blocks. Soon, they were busy building in a corner, giving each other instructions in a language reserved for only the two of them.

Mr. Pearson watched Jasmine and Mrs. Carwall, as well as the speech therapist and the boys' mother, work on their IEP (Individualized Education Program) together, just as most of them had no doubt worked on the IFSP (Individualized Family Service Plan) two years before, and he thought of what a need was being met. His grandfather had coped his whole life with a speech impediment which may have been corrected if early intervention had been an option in his day.

"We've come a long way," thought Mr. Pearson as he shook hands with the little family before their departure. Then he headed back to his office where the central office observation team was waiting to descend on his classrooms, intimidating his hardworking teachers with their uninvited presence.

"And we've got a long way to go," Mr. Pearson heard himself say.

REFLECTIONS

1. What concepts from the early intervention model might we learn from and use at all grade levels?
2. What are the benefits for children when their parents and teachers collaborate?
3. How can we respond with sensitivity to the economic differences between ourselves and the people we serve?

SOLUTIONS

Seamless transitions are always a worthy goal as schools escort children across the thresholds of their development. Thanks to Part C of IDEA, the Individuals with Disabilities Education Act, trained and competent professionals are now waiting to join hands with parents of high-risk infants and toddlers in an effort to give them a head start that could level the playing field. (Over three hundred thousand children from birth through age two were served in 2013 alone, through early intervention services across the fifty states and beyond, as a result of the evidence that children's brains develop significantly in the first three years of life.[1]) On the child's third birthday, the day he or she ages out of the early intervention program, he or she is eligible to enter a public preschool classroom tuition free. There, his or her therapeutic services, such as speech, physical therapy, and occupational therapy, will be continued.

The importance of informing the public of these services, as well as collaborating with families, has never been more widely recognized as critical to the success of children. It is crucial that we convey to teacher candidates in their training years that in order to reach the child, they will need to be prepared to embrace the family. There are few things the teacher could do that would have a greater impact on the child's school experience from the sandbox to the graduation march and beyond.

NOTE

1. Excerpt from the Facebook page of a college student (and former high school valedictorian) who was once serviced as a three-year-old in a Kentucky public preschool program. Her IEP had called for speech and language therapy. These reflections were posted after a week volunteering at a summer camp for adults with special needs (reprinted with permission).

> A week ago today I first met the adults who would have an impact on me I will never forget. The world refers to them as special needs or a little different from us, but they seem to have discovered the most important aspects of life that we do not cherish. Their constant laughter that demonstrated their pure joy, their genuine apologies that showed their desire for forgiveness, their random kisses that displayed their undeniable love, their generous gifts that revealed their selflessness, and their helping hands that proved their friendship touched me so deeply. God desires us to have faith like a child, the simplicity and pureness that they hold, and these precious adults illustrated to me what that looks like. Their beautiful smiles, shrill laughter, funny senses of humor, and sweet words remind me that the

simple things in life are the most valuable. My words cannot do justice to how much these beautiful individuals blessed me, but I can say that in those moments with them, I felt as if I had touched my God.

TWO

Cinderella

NAEYC STANDARD 1: PROMOTING CHILD DEVELOPMENT
AND LEARNING

1b: Knowing and Understanding the Multiple Influences on Early Development and Learning

Mrs. Hughes found herself rereading the article in the Sunday paper. It wasn't the article (though chilling in itself), as much as the accompanying photo, that pulled her in. She had seen those eyes before. Foul play was suspected in the untimely death of Wanda Hillard, a young mother of four, over on Stella Ridge.

Even at the tender age of twenty-nine, the ravages of poverty were written on the haunting face: missing teeth, wrinkles beyond her years, gray, stringy hair, and that defeated look in her eyes.

She had seen that look before. Mrs. Hughes felt her own eyes mist as a little face from long ago came into focus. It was her first year of teaching. She got the class nobody wanted. Too many kids—thirty-something of them—with issues, too many to count. As she tried to manage all the problems that clamored for her attention, the noisiest problems took priority.

Wanda was not a noisy problem.

In fact, she was one of the most withdrawn children Mrs. Hughes ever ran across in over twenty years of teaching. There was no mommy. There was a daddy who Mrs. Hughes never got to meet, and lots of younger siblings. Once, the principal had asked her to question Wanda. One of the

7

parents had called with concerns, he explained. Could Mrs. Hughes (at the time young Miss Grayson) talk to her and see if there was anything "not normal" between Wanda and her daddy?

Miss Grayson had tried. But Wanda was a closed well, the lid tightly lodged. There was no prying it open; not even a crack.

If only there had been more time. If Wanda was in her class today, Mrs. Hughes would have found a way. She would have had a cozy corner with soft books and pretty dolls, where a little girl could escape from the cruel reality of her childhood.

She would have taught all of the little girls (and boys) that they were princesses (and princes), born for royalty, and that nobody, *nobody*, no matter who they were, should ever, ever . . .

She would have been safe. A safe teacher Wanda could run to. She wouldn't have been so upset all the time with all of the misbehavior, the confusion, and the demands. Losing her temper. Shouting threats. All of her desperate attempts to manage a class that needed a veteran teacher — not the new kid on the block.

She would have found a way to see past her jungle to the wallflower.

Mrs. Hughes wiped her eyes and folded the newspaper. She had been meaning to clean out the attic ever since the kids got big. Perhaps there was an old Cinderella book in the mix. And a dress-up chest from which a little girl could don lacy, white gloves and a flowing gown.

She picked up the phone book and looked for the local shelter for women. They had a really good spokesperson there who went to schools and did talks for kids about appropriate touching. She highlighted the phone number to call first thing Monday morning. And it was time to commit to memory the number to the Child Protection Services. It was always a pain to have to dig that number up, while the students were competing for her attention.

But for now, this lump in her throat had to be dealt with. Mrs. Hughes went to her bedroom, got on her knees, and had a good cry. She wept for all the little Wandas who had passed through her classroom, their secret unnoticed — some withdrawn like this child, some acting out, much harder to love. "Open my eyes and ears," she prayed. "Don't let me miss another one."

Mrs. Hughes did not expect the chain of events that was to follow. Mr. Hillard's trial and imprisonment. The four Hillard children taken in by an aunt who lived in her school precinct. And the youngest child's name on her roster in the fall.

As the fair-skinned youngster, her little head covered with tangled, blond curls and her bare legs eaten up with bugbites, entered her class-room that first day, Mrs. Hughes felt her heart skip a beat. She couldn't have felt more privileged if she had been called back for a tryout on Broadway. Sweet second chance.

While the other children spread their elaborate school supplies out on their desks and hung up their new-smelling backpacks, Tilly knelt beside her desk and took a used, spiral-bound notebook out of her stained back-pack, which smelled strongly of cigarette smoke.

Mrs. Hughes bent down beside her. Tilly avoided eye contact, as her mother had always done. Mrs. Hughes spoke softly, "Tilly, I like your name. My name is Mrs. Hughes. I was noticing how you follow the rules so well. I wonder if you would be my line leader for today?"

A nod of the tangled curls and Tilly was in her seat, looking down at her desk.

"Well, class," said Mrs. Hughes, when the parents had kissed their children good-bye. "If you'll come calmly to the rug, I have a book I'd like to share with you."

The children eagerly scrambled for the rug.

Mrs. Hughes noticed that Tilly took a spot quietly at the back of the rug, perhaps hoping to blend into the wall, like a flower. . . .

Mrs. Hughes smiled to herself and pictured the day when this little princess would inch close enough to be taken up into her arms for story time. For today, Mrs. Hughes was content to bide her time, speaking softly, giving affirmation. . . . "Joey, thank you for being a good listener." "Sarah, that's a good point. But let's remember to wait until Jessica is finished speaking." "Now, I have a story I want to share with all of you. . . . Once upon a time, in a land far, far away, there was a lonely, lovely girl named Cinderella . . ."

THROUGH HIS EYES

When Mr. Pearson walked back down the hall toward his office, not knowing how to respond to his own feelings of immense emotion after seeing Mrs. Hughes cry tears of joy over second chances, he reached for his keys. He still had paperwork to do, and it was only 4 p.m., but he needed to just get home as fast as he could to his own girls.

There they were in the yard playing, and anxiously awaiting their hero to come home for supper.

"Daddy's home!" Mr. Pearson heard them yell to their mommy on the porch as he got out of his truck.

"You're home early today, Honey," Mrs. Pearson smiled and waved as she watered her ferns.

He tried to not reveal that he had been crying, but she could tell. "Jack, what's bothering you?"

He walked up on the porch and gave her a long hug, then simply said, "I love you. And I love these girls. If I don't tell you all that enough, I'm sorry."

"Well, mercy me, what brought that on? We know you love us, Honey. You're a wonderful husband, you're a great father, and you're a good provider. Our home wouldn't be a home without you."

"But I could do better. I take you all for granted, and I never want to do that anymore. Today, a new student came to school that one of my teachers felt a strong kinship to. You see, this little girl has been raised in poverty. And her mother was murdered over the weekend. My teacher had her mom in school twenty years ago, and seeing this child overwhelmed her with memories. As a young teacher, she suspected that this student's mom was being abused as a little girl by her own father all those years ago, but didn't know what to do."

"Well, in reality, what could she have done?"

"Nothing, or so it seems. No matter how hard we try, our hands are tied by the legal system. But, it all just hit me in the face as I realized how blessed I am to have you and our three precious girls. We're the privileged ones. We, to these unfortunate children of poverty, are like kings and queens. They don't ever get to live in our world. Sometimes, they don't even make it to their thirtieth birthday here on this earth."

"I know Jack, I know. But down at the school every day, you and your staff are trying everything you can think of to help these kids get out of that cycle of poverty, drugs, and crime, and who knows what else goes on in their homes in the dead of night. And some do indeed make it out. Remember Billy? No one in this town gave him any chance of doing something with his life, and now he's a pastor, and his wife is a professor at the university. Because you all care, some do make it."

"But not Tilly's mom."

"Honey, you've got to let that go. There's nothing you can do about it."

"Maybe there is. Tilly's papaw is still around. And I'll go have a long talk with the sheriff first thing in the morning. Perhaps we can save this one."

"I knew you were going to say that. All I can say is keep doing what your heart tells you to do, Jack. Then, you can always come home from school and sleep well at night."

"And my heart's telling me right now to take my lovely wife and sweet daughters out to the lake with a bucket of fried chicken, and then get milkshakes for dessert on the way home. How's that sound?"

As his girls squealed, having heard their daddy's plans for the evening, they didn't see him slip into the bedroom and fall to his knees. "Oh, dear God in heaven, thank you for this treasure you've given me—my family. Help me to get it right. Thank you for these precious women in my life. Please, please . . . help me to get it right. And may I never, ever give up on standing in the gap for those less fortunate—those innocent souls at school who You entrust to my care. I realize that if miracles are to happen in their lives, they may need to begin with me."

REFLECTIONS

1. How aggressive is your school and community in addressing suspected child abuse?
2. How detailed and thorough is the training you receive on how to recognize and report child abuse, and how to provide support for victims in your classroom?
3. What student or parent you currently know is most likely in an abusive situation at home? What are you going to do about it?

SOLUTIONS

According to data from the National Child Abuse and Neglect Data System (NCANDS), a nationally estimated 1,640 children died from abuse and neglect in 2012. This translates to an average of four children in the United States dying every day from abuse or neglect.

Nearly all fifty states have definitions of the different types of abuse and neglect. They can be accessed at the Child Welfare Information Gateway website, www.childwelfare.gov, by searching the state statutes. The definitions generally include physical, emotional, and sexual abuse, as well as neglect and abandonment.

Kentucky, for example, defines *neglect* as "inadequate or dangerous childrearing practices" and includes in its list:

1. Lack of proper supervision
2. Failure to see that child attends school
3. Denial of necessities of life, e.g., food, water, clothing
4. Denial of medical treatment
5. Abandonment, malnutrition, failure to thrive

Physical abuse is defined as "the infliction of injury, other than by accidental means, on a child by another person."

Sexual abuse refers to "sexual assault or exploitation of a minor by an adult, or between two children when one of the children is significantly older or there is a significant power differential between the children, or when coercion is used." The examples include prostitution, exploitation, or involvement of child in pornography.

Psychological or emotional abuse occurs when an adult conveys to a child that the child is endangered, unsafe, worthless, unwanted, or damaged. It may include verbal threats, terrorization, isolation, or frequent berating of a child by the adult.

In many states, any citizen who suspects abuse or neglect is required by law to report it. In all states, teachers are required to report suspicions. The national child abuse hotline number is 1-800-4-A-Child or 1-800-422-4453.

In Henry Cloud's book, *Necessary Endings* (2010), he stresses the critical importance of embracing the need for change, and then taking the appropriate steps to realize the various "new beginnings" that can come our way in life. This principle is also true for organizations. And as educators, we too often assume someone else is going to fix the human brokenness we experience with various aspects of our job.

In regard to the numerous incidents of child abuse which we suspect or know are going on in the homes of many of our students, looking the other way and expecting social service agencies to perform miracles is naive indeed. Instead, an individual school, or better yet, a school district, could easily form a task force to specifically focus on the victims of child abuse in the school community.

Perhaps a more aggressive advocacy for the children entrusted to our care would lead to social agencies and the judicial system taking a stronger stand. Perhaps volunteers would get more involved in mentoring and providing support for our at-risk students at school. Perhaps faculties would begin to become more enraged about the abuse of innocent children if the issue was kept front and center.

But also, a school or school district would see a difference over time if character education and the teaching of human values were given more "voice" in the curriculum. Generationally, a community's culture would change. We've all heard our grandparents or others from the mid-twentieth century talk about how in school they were held to a high standard of how to be responsible citizens who would give back to society in positive ways. Have we even taught servant leadership in our schools in recent years? Or, have we brought upon ourselves a sense of entitlement that permeates our social classes and leads to more and more adults disrespecting children as never before?

Oh, what a difference one school could make!

THREE

The Wheels on the Bus

NAEYC STANDARD 4: USING DEVELOPMENTALLY EFFECTIVE
APPROACHES TO CONNECT WITH CHILDREN AND FAMILIES

4a: Understanding Positive Relationships and Supportive Interactions as the Foundation of Their Work with Young Children

Her name was Annabelle, and she was tired. But her calling to serve children was not yet finished, so after raising a houseful of them—some hers by birth and others by adoption, and after burying her childhood sweetheart, her lifelong companion—she heard a still, small voice say, "Go back to the schools. The children need you."

The directions were clear. But there were a few roadblocks ahead. At sixty-three, she had no desire to start the process to becoming a teacher, her body was too tired to be a janitor, the instructional aides' waiting list was thirty miles long, and she had cooked so many meals for her army over the years that the thought of cooking for a school made her sigh . . . but they needed bus drivers. That's what they told her. And Annabelle knew the area—every nook and cranny of this little county she had lived in and loved for over six decades.

She listened again for the still, small voice. "Go back to the schools. The children need you." She studied and earned her CDL. Then she put in her application.

By March, she was on the substitute bus drivers' list. In August, the district garage gave her a bus—Number 39—and a route of her own. She sat behind the wheel of her very own school bus, its body seeming as big as a freight train, and wept. The words from a song her children had learned at school came floating into her memory. "The wheels on the bus go 'round and 'round, 'round and 'round, 'round and 'round. The wheels on the bus go 'round and 'round, all through the town."

The air was dewy the morning she set out to pick up her first run, and she smelled school mornings from years past as she drove by the honeysuckle bushes along Highway 55. A small girl in pigtails and a bigger boy in baggy pants and—*what do they call those? "chucks"*—were waiting at her first stop.

"Good morning, children," smiled Annabelle as her little charge mounted the steps.

The children nodded at this strange, new bus driver.

But Annabelle was not a stranger for long. By October, most of the children had adopted her as a grandmother. They had come to count on her warm greeting, her positive regard for them, and her firm rules.

Annabelle was uncomplicated because she didn't know about the race. She didn't know about the race because they put her at the end of the line. In Annabelle's case, it was the best place to be.

Each afternoon, while Annabelle waited for the other buses to load, she watched in wonder as the wiggly lines of children hurried out of the school. How Annabelle loved the children. Sometimes the voice would tell her, "This one's in trouble," or, "Lift that one up to the throne." With tears streaming down her cheeks, Annabelle would intercede for the children.

She definitely had an advantage. Annabelle liked to wait. There was no one to rush home to; none of the same stresses of younger bus drivers with mouths to feed and bills to pay. (On Sundays, there were precious grandchildren, a houseful of them, and her quiver was full. But for the rest of the week, there was just Anabelle.) So she wouldn't have needed to race even if she had known . . . about the race.

One day, she did see a harried, young teacher rushing a child out the school door, late. The child was trembling; the teacher's face was white. But they were too late. The bus's door had been shut. And as the teacher stood waving frantically and the child looking imploringly through the glass door, the bus rolled away. Annabelle honked at the driver in front of her, but the bus before her only picked up speed. Annabelle leaned out her own door and called to the worried, little pair, "Are you all right, children?"

The young teacher's angry face melted at the kind words, and she blinked back tears. "We'll go to the office and call your daddy," she said softly to the girl beside her. "We're all right—thank you, Ma'am," she said to Annabelle.

Though the job made Annabelle nostalgic, she was diligent not to let her mind wander when she rolled up to pick up that first child each day. From that moment until the moment she had delivered the last one safely home, she was at attention, all eyes, all ears, keenly aware of the enormous responsibility placed trustingly on her bent shoulders.

Sometimes, when she would walk her bus in the evening, Annabelle would pause at a seat. "This is where Norman always sits," she would whisper. She would place her leathery hands on the back of the seat, and in her mind she would take Norman up on her lap. Norman, the insolent, troubled teenager. Like the troublemaker described in the Proverbs, he was constantly communicating to his partners with winking eyes and signaling fingers. What had happened to produce such an angry, defiant young man? Annabelle shuddered to think what Norman went home to every day. So, in her mind, she held him on her lap. In her mind, she wept tears over that overgrown boy, as a mother would have wept over him, had Norman had a mother.

There was no time for the race.

Another time, Annabelle had to blink hard to make sure her eyes weren't deceiving her. As the lineup of buses was once again waiting to load the children after school, a teacher brought a tiny child out ahead of the other children to catch the bus in front of Annabelle's. This wasn't the bus stop, but it was easy to follow the teacher's reasoning. The children in line were chomping at the bit to get on that bus. As soon as their bus pulled up, the competition would be strong, and a small child could easily get trampled.

But apparently, the bus driver in front of her didn't see it that way. As the little one—he couldn't have been over three and a half—was climbing the steps, and the teacher was reaching into the bus adjusting his backpack on his little shoulders, the bus door suddenly shut, and the bus lurched forward—to the real stop.

Annabelle drew in a sharp breath. The teacher marched to the bus and got on with the children. Annabelle did not hear the conversation inside, but she knew it was not a happy one.

It was a puzzling thing, Annabelle thought. There seemed to be such a small window of time in which the teachers were allowed to load the buses. If they got there too early (while some of the bus drivers were visiting outside the buses), the teachers had to keep the children waiting in the heat or cold. But if they got there a minute too late, the race was on. . . . Annabelle had raised enough children to remember how stressful dismissal time was inside a big school, getting all the small children sorted out to their various destinations. A little patience from all the team members would have gone a long way. After all, they were all on the same team, weren't they?

Annabelle thought of all the caring bus drivers she had known over the years. She thought of her own dear husband, God rest his soul, who had pulled the bus over to tell the big boys why chewing tobacco was harmful to them—and in the same monologue had invited them to the Pony League baseball tryouts on Saturday. "I'll make sure you get picked up by my team," he promised.

She thought of the fine young bus driver four buses ahead of her who had called the child protection services over a small girl whose parents often failed to be home to receive her. Annabelle knew in her heart they weren't all in the race.

"The wheels on the bus go 'round and 'round, 'round and 'round, 'round and 'round," Annabelle hummed on the last day of school as she pulled Number 39 into her yard after a sweltering ride home. She walked the bus, checking each seat; even stooping her arthritic knees to check under seats—you never know—one could have fallen asleep and slid underneath. She pushed the windows up. What a hot day for early June! How joyful the children's good-byes had been for the summer. . . .

As Annabelle turned to walk back to the front of the bus, she noticed a paper trapped in a window. Annabelle pulled it out to wad it up, and the large, sprawling words "to miss ana bell" caught her eye. Curiously, Annabelle unfolded the wrinkled note: "i will miss you, mis ana bell."

How long the voice would keep sending her back she could not tell. One thing was for sure. She had time to wait. And she would always make the decision not to know about the race.

THROUGH HIS EYES

As the cars rolled in one by one, Mr. Pearson chuckled to himself. "First time all year they will all have made it to a meeting on time."

This was the annual staff picnic at his farm, always held the afternoon of the last day of spring term, just after the kids were dismissed for the summer.

As might be expected, this was always a celebrative event, and Mr. Pearson grinned with pride as he stood over the grill, turning hamburgers while his wife brought out food from the kitchen. "Here comes your team, honey."

"Yep, here come the escapees from the asylum."

"You all survived another year," she quipped. A couple of the first to arrive heard the lighthearted exchange and laughed in agreement. By the last day of school, survival was a good way to put it.

"Okay, everybody, gather 'round and start filling your plates! Then, I have my annual awards to give out!" Mr. Pearson yelled loudly so all could hear, as the yard was quickly filling with people. He always invited the entire staff, including cafeteria crew, custodians, and bus drivers. This was the one time all year that they all were duty-free at the same time. He made it a point to encourage them to bring their families along, too.

After an hour or so of good eats, laughing, telling funny stories, and just plain, old chilling out in celebration of the beginning of summer, Mr. Pearson asked for everyone's attention by clanking an old skillet with a spoon.

"Well, as is our custom, today we want to wrap up another wonderful school year by passing out a few awards."

A lighthearted murmur rippled through the crowd as most everyone knew what was coming—lots of poking fun and some mock awards that were sure to single out some notoriously curious behavior by members of the staff at some time during the year. And, sure enough, Mr. Pearson did not disappoint.

But, as he got to the end of his list, and all the certificates were gone, he reached under the table and pulled out a beautiful black and gold plaque. The inscription on the front simply read, "Uncommon Love for Our Children—Staff Person of the Year—Annabelle Delong."

As Annabelle sat in her lawn chair in disbelief, Mr. Pearson shared this testimony to one person's greatness.

"I never dreamed when I was introduced last July to our newest bus driver, who our transportation director simply referred to as 'Ms. Annabelle,' what a positive impact this one little lady would have on our school. But I soon started figuring it out. From her very first day on her route, way back there in early August, when I'm sure she was as nervous as nervous can be, I began receiving phone calls of appreciation from parents, grandparents, and even others in the community. They all said the same thing: 'Ms. Annabelle sure does do an especially good job of taking care of our children.'"

"And at school, it seemed that every day another child would come and report to me something kind that Annabelle had done on the bus. And my teachers, oh my—how they so appreciated Annabelle taking the time to greet them, and chat with them, and to patiently wait for their children during those hectic, frantic dismissals at the end of the day."

"On one occasion, a few weeks ago, I even received a phone call from our superintendent, who had been getting daily complaints about one of our drivers and how he was so rude, and in too much of a hurry. Sadly, this driver was dismissed from his job later that week. But guess who the superintendent suggested I put on the longest, roughest run for the rest of the year?"

"You're right—Annabelle. The super simply said, 'And find me as many more 'Annabelles' as you can anytime we have a bus driver position open. I want her to be the new model of customer service in our district. And, I want her to help me train all our drivers from this point on. So, when school's out, have her come over to my office. I need to talk to her. I want to know more about this lady of smiles and goodness; this lady who actually inspires people to call in here to my office with good reports instead of complaints.'"

Annabelle was visibly moved, and held a handkerchief to her eyes as Mr. Pearson capped off his presentation. "Join me in congratulating our staff person of the year . . . Ms. Annabelle Delong."

Annabelle stood, and everyone else stood too, giving her the longest ovation she'd ever seen. After what seemed like five minutes of applause, she spoke softly, "I don't know what to say. This is all I know to do—to be kind to people."

The picnic went on, for hours and hours. No one seemed to want to leave that day. Mr. Pearson thought to himself, "From now on, I am only looking for more Annabelles. This is how we will build the best school in the state. It's almost too simple, but it's true. Genuinely and lovingly taking care of kids, and each other . . . this is what we do. This is what parents, the school board, and the community assume we know how to do. So, we will—from this point on."

Mr. Pearson smiled, and later, had the best night's sleep he'd had in years.

REFLECTIONS

1. Can you remember your favorite secretary, bus driver, custodian, or cafeteria worker from your childhood days in school?
2. Why were they so well-liked by students?
3. Are the most influential leaders only the principal and others with the official title of "leader"?

SOLUTIONS

In *Transforming School Culture*, Anthony Muhammad (2009) zeroes in on "beneath the surface" issues that cripple schools. He emphasizes that a typical school will have teachers who sabotage the efforts of others. What results is a preoccupation with how the teachers feel, who is mad at whom, who is getting their way, and so on. Sadly, in this emotionally charged and distrustful environment, what is left out of the mix is the critical work that is being done by the non-instructional staff—those who day after day are taking care of the students and adding great value to the school's menu of services.

Schools that have leadership who recognize this reality and who build in specific praise and recognition for the many adults who are playing a part in adding to the total umbrella of student support, are building a strong culture that values *everyone* who is a part of the school community. And, this belief in all who are serving can build such a strong ambiance of "community" that it helps drown out the naysayers who tear down by creating a toxic culture.

To further illustrate the importance of feeling valued and finding meaning in one's work, in his bestselling book, *Drive*, Daniel Pink (2009) describes the "purpose motive," a force that is moving to front and center in the priorities of the Baby Boomer generation as they reach their sixtieth birthday and beyond. Organizations are noticing a sharp rise in volunteerism in the work force, confirming the theory that volunteer work is nourishing people in ways that paid work is not.

In the same chapter, Pink writes that typical management words like "efficiency, focus, and differentiation" fail to rouse human hearts in the same way words representing deeper ideals do, such as "honor, truth, love, justice, and beauty."

As this relates to our schools, though conversations on test scores and accountability must take place, those are not what give teachers and staff the type of purpose that changes children's lives. Bringing in inspiring keynote speakers does. Affirming individual teachers and staff for their specific gifts and graces does. Caring enough about these stressed professionals to sponsor them for a weekend retreat of rest and renewal would. If we spent at least as many professional development hours inspiring teachers to be heroes in the lives of our children as we do reminding them that it all comes down to the percentile in the last column, teachers' work would be more fulfilling and rewarding, and they wouldn't have their life's worth laid in the balance by the test scores printed on the front page of the Sunday paper . . . and found wanting.

FOUR

Poster Child

1c: Using Developmental Knowledge to Create Healthy, Respectful, Supportive, and Challenging Learning Environments for Young Children

He could have been the poster child for dysfunctional families. Or ADHD. Or drug babies.

But he didn't know it. He just knew he couldn't make his mouth hush even when it was getting him in trouble; he had to fight when people stepped on him; and he loved Jesus.

Mrs. Sweeney cared about him. He knew that, too. He loved her attention, something he had never been able to inspire from anybody at home. No matter how good or bad or irresistible he tried to be.

Mrs. Sweeney was different. She said something nice to him about himself every day. Whether it was that his handwriting was improving, or he was being a good neighbor, or she was glad he was in her class. Most of the time, though, he was busy making her not glad that he was in her class.

He didn't know why he did it. He just couldn't help himself. His body couldn't control his tongue, his energy, his outbursts, his anger. And besides, he got way more attention by being bad than being good.

For example, when Mrs. Sweeney was teaching math, she had to give everybody her attention at the same time. So she wrote things on the board and talked about them to the whole group. Ethan hated that. It was long, way longer than he could endure. So he found ways to get Mrs. Sweeney's attention then, too. And all the time.

He interrupted. He whined. When corrected, he threw fits. He provoked other children. When they fought back, he got physical. When Mr. Pearson was brought into the picture, that was even better; even more attention, and this time from a man—a gender which was certainly missing from his life anywhere else.

And he loved Jesus. It was because when people talked about Jesus, that leveled the playing field. They all seemed to agree that Jesus liked everybody—good, bad, or both. From the stories they told him in Sunday school, there were no favorites with this guy; not the well-dressed kids who smelled nice, or the smart ones, or the ones who could control their bodies and their words and their anger.

He had picked up back in kindergarten that school teachers didn't teach as much about Jesus. They focused more on Abraham Lincoln, and Christopher Columbus, and Santa Claus. But if you brought His name up, they all knew who He was. Some of them tried not to show that they knew. They just got tight-lipped, which proved they did know and were trying not to talk about it. But most of them got kind of gentle, like people do when you mention your grandpa, or Mother Teresa (or Abraham Lincoln), even if they have just finished bawling you out.

And Mrs. Sweeney answered your questions. Even if you talked about things you shouldn't talk about in school, like the real meaning of Easter. Mrs. Sweeney often prefaced her answers with things like, "Not everyone believes the same things, but Christians believe . . ." and she would explain what Christians believe.

So it shouldn't have been such a big surprise (the pamphlets) to Mrs. Sweeney, of all people. But it was . . .

He could have been the poster child for dysfunctional families. Or ADHD. Or drug babies. By October, Mrs. Sweeney had called social services three times. The guidance counselor came and got her from the gym during the attendance rally. The social worker was waiting in the office. He needed to talk to Ethan, but first he wanted to talk to her. He knew Ethan's whole family on a first name basis. Everyone knew the parents were into drugs, but they were slick, he said, really slick.

Many days, most days, Mrs. Sweeney's emotions ran the full gamut when it came to this child. She wanted to give him a good scrubbing and cook him a breakfast fit for a king when he came in the mornings, dirty and hungry. She wanted to spank him for continuously interrupting while she tried to teach the class, for picking fights, and for mocking her when she lost her cool. And as she watched him struggle day after day over the same words in his reading book, she wanted to take him up in her arms and rock him. "It wasn't supposed to be this way," she wanted to whisper in his ear. "And you're a smart little boy. You are smart. I promise."

He had a gift for music. His rhythm. His voice. She first noticed his ear for music the day she brought her keyboard to class. After she played "Mary Had a Little Lamb" for her appreciative audience, Ethan insisted on playing a tune. She expected him to pluck around on the keys, but not to play back to her the very tune she had just played, note for note.

A hush fell over the little group, and then Collins said, "You're a good player, Ethan."

And so he was. Mrs. Sweeney tried hard to get the music teacher to celebrate Ethan's talent. "How did Ethan do today in music class?" she would ask often when she picked the children up from music. "I bet he would make a fine soloist for the Christmas program."

But Mrs. Elliot never picked up on any of her hints, and finally one day, Mrs. Elliot explained, "I just don't see it. What I see is a child who will not behave or cooperate."

Mrs. Sweeney looked at her, speechless for a moment. But then she found her tongue, "If you don't see it, Mrs. Elliot, then that's a tragedy indeed. You hold in your nimble hands the power to rescue a child like Ethan. Come along, children."

It was an uphill climb, this battle to restore Ethan's reputation. It might have helped if he would have cooperated in the matter.

By March, it was clear that Ethan was going to be with her for another year. She used every resource she could find to spur him on: the Reading Recovery teacher, homemade phonics games, the family resource center's tutor, compelling learning activities on the computer. And anybody's instructional aide that she could borrow for a few minutes here and there.

By April, she was at the end of her patience with Ethan's behavior. So she used her last card—holding the end-of-the-year field trip over his head for leverage. It didn't work. Ethan had lost his field trip before they even got the behavior contracts sent home.

His uncle dropped him off, tardy, at the front door, as his class was waiting in the breezeway for the field trip bus. Mrs. Sweeney went to

Ethan—he was all sleepy-eyed and tousle-haired—and laid her hand gently on his shoulder. "Ethan, Mrs. Day is waiting for you in the library. I've left you some seatwork with her."

"Okay, Mrs. Sweeney," he said, and she watched him shuffle down the hall to the library, his torn backpack slung over his shoulder. She wanted to run after him and say, "Uh, Ethan, there's been a change in plans. We're taking you on the field trip after all." But rules were rules, and the bus was pulling up. She took her line leader's hand and made another backward glance as Ethan opened the library door. Mrs. Day wouldn't know he hadn't had his breakfast.

Next year would be easier . . . it always was. The second grade would be easier for Ethan the next time around, and he would be a leader in the class this time. She would make a big deal out of his knowing the ropes, and she would send him on errands, and let him help his younger classmates. She would do everything in her power to try to make up for the huge gash retention leaves in a child's self-esteem. Years later, you can overhear them telling their classmates, "I'm in the eighth grade, but I'm supposed to be in the ninth." They never forget.

The last day of school arrived long overdue, as eagerly anticipated as a Christmas morning. Mrs. Sweeney played some games with her class, showed movies, extended their recess, and passed out popsicles. As the second-run bus riders were going out the door, Ethan turned and put some crumpled pamphlets into Mrs. Sweeney's hands. "Would you pass these out to the other teachers?" he asked.

Mrs. Sweeney read the title, "You Were Meant for Eden." So her budding musician was also an evangelist.

Ethan looked back at her as his group was rushing out the door.

"I'll see that they get them, Ethan," she promised. "Have a good summer. I'll see you next year."

"Have a good summer, Mrs. Sweeney."

"Ethan, I love you."

Ethan's face exploded into a huge smile. "I'll see you next year, Mrs. Sweeney!" he called.

Mrs. Sweeney turned to go into her classroom. She stopped suddenly and turned back.

"Oh, by the way," she said to her pod partners, who were mingling outside their classroom doors. "Ethan wanted me to pass these out."

Her pod partners chuckled. "Ethan, of all people," said one of them.

"His story isn't finished yet," said Mrs. Sweeney gently.

He could have been the poster child for dysfunctional families. Or ADHD. Or drug babies. One sad day, he would understand that. But for today, he was Ethan. The playing field was leveled. And Mrs. Sweeney loved him.

THROUGH HIS EYES

As the buses pulled out of the school parking lot, Mr. Pearson breathed a sigh of relief. He could feel the tension leaving his shoulders before he even made it to the library—where his staff was having a lunch and retirement party for one of his veteran teachers. He loved his work, but he also became physically and emotionally exhausted by the time June 1 rolled around.

As he turned the corner by the lunchroom, he overheard Mrs. Sweeney bragging on her little Ethan to Mrs. Robbins—the teacher who was retiring. "Yes, Ethan is one of our recovery projects," he thought to himself. And he was full of pride as he so appreciated how his staff truly did love these kids.

During the retirement celebration, when Mrs. Robbins came up front to speak to her colleagues, there was soon not a dry eye in the house.

"I am going to miss you folks . . . my dedicated and talented colleagues. To be honest, I have dreaded this day for a long time. But I am nearing sixty years old, and my body just can't handle the daily grind of running a classroom anymore. But, oh let me tell you, what a wonderful ride it has been. My first year as a teacher, I was just twenty-one years old, and the kids have been the passion of my life. I don't know what I'll do this August, when the fall term begins, and I won't be here with you as you get your rooms ready and start up a brand-new school year."

As Mr. Pearson stood up to speak and to give Mrs. Robbins a special plaque from the school, he realized that he was losing one of the pillars of this school community. His voice broke as he shared what a joy and privilege it had been to work with her day after day, to observe how wise and gentle she was in parent conferences, and how her students hovered around her as if she were their grandmother.

When he glanced over toward Mrs. Sweeney, she nodded with a tearful smile, and Mr. Pearson experienced one of those epiphany moments that don't come along very often. But when they do, they're like music from Heaven.

"And, uh, Mrs. Robbins, one more thing. I've been thinking about a lot of new possibilities as I've been working out details for this coming fall's roster. Well, it seems we've got a dilemma. You see, Mrs. Sweeney has a very special little boy in her room who we're going to have to keep back for another year. His name's Ethan and he is absolutely precious. Well, as it turns out, Mrs. Sweeney asked me just a couple of days ago if I knew of anyone who would be available to come in and volunteer as her special assistant to help Ethan a couple of mornings a week . . . "

Mrs. Robbins's eyes welled up with tears, and she rushed up to hug her principal's neck before he could extend the offer for her to think about over the summer.

"I don't need to think about it. I'd love to! Thank you, thank you, thank you . . . I don't really have to retire after all, do I?"

"No Ma'am, you sure don't." Mr. Pearson looked over at Mrs. Sweeney, and winked with a smile that simply said, "Thank you. Such a great idea."

Everybody clapped loudly, the party went on for two more hours, and a little boy's odds went way, way up.

REFLECTIONS

1. Does your school have a volunteer mentor program?
2. Are retired teachers invited to participate in volunteering at school to work with at-risk students?
3. Does your school have a holistic liberal arts curriculum, with an array of art, music, physical education, and other extended curriculum opportunities?

SOLUTIONS

In *Creating Leaderful Organizations* (Raelin 2003), how to bring out leadership in everyone is explored. This new paradigm is gaining momentum, as leaders in all organizations are realizing that the limitless potential of the collective whole of human resources is so much greater.

In any school community, there is a priceless resource which is too often overlooked—our retirees who still want to be involved in using their talents to give back. In this age of budget uncertainties and cut-backs, these veterans of education, business, health care, and an array of other fields have the potential to make a huge difference in the effectiveness of the local school, and in the lives of the students it serves.

But, in reality, have we tapped into this abundance of human capital? Do we find ourselves asking for volunteers to assist with field trips, mentoring programs, tutoring, co-teaching, sponsoring clubs, presenting guest lectures . . . yet forgetting to invite our retired professionals to become partners with us?

Today, in thinking about the needs of the school for the upcoming semester, a principal who will take the time to make some phone calls, do some home visits, and schedule an informational meeting will soon find that he or she has access to an incredible "adjunct faculty" of skilled volunteers who can become that missing piece in putting together a great school which meets the varying needs of all of its students.

And due to the rise of drug abuse among parents as well as the increased incidence of ADHD among children, that variety of needs in students is more complex than ever before. More and more babies are born addicted. Not only can this impact their brain development, often compromising impulse control, but being raised by parents abusing drugs tends to lead to neglect and trauma. Any neglect severe enough to be an insult to the system can have the same impact as trauma on the brain's development. Just as clogged arteries can motivate the heart to form new pathways, a traumatized brain develops differently than the typical brain, and this can impact behavior in negative ways.

Another challenging disorder for an increasing number of children in our society is ADHD (Attention Deficit Hyperactivity Disorder). There are many theories as to why the incidence of this disorder is on the rise. Children receive fewer opportunities to get exercise and fresh air, they spend a large percentage of time on electronics, our diets include many unhealthy additives, and five-year-olds are not wired to sit at a desk for six hours. Those are four significant factors in our culture which were not with us as recently as a couple of generations ago.

So our schools have their work cut out for them. We must find ways to meet the needs of traumatized children and to educate parents on the importance of a healthy lifestyle for all, while making the school environment healthier as well. This is a challenge in light of the fact that the pressure to perform on standardized tests has trickled down as low as kindergarten and is now hovering over the preschool setting.

It will take teamwork and honest self-reflection to combat these challenges of our time in an effective way so we can meet the needs of our young ones suffering from the fallout.

FIVE

Moonlighting

NAEYC STANDARD : USING DEVELOPMENTALLY EFFECTIVE
APPROACHES TO CONNECT WITH CHILDREN AND FAMILIES

4d: Reflecting on Own Practice to Promote Positive Outcomes for Each Child

He taught a couple of night classes over at the local college, mostly for his sanity. It must have been one of those weeks when his third graders were responding to either the pull of a full moon on the earth's gravity, or a cold front moving in, or rain . . . when he filled out the application.

Most of his career, he had had a love/hate relationship with teaching. He loved June through August. He hated the rest of the year. (No, to be fair, there had been good moments—good days, good weeks, even good years). But Mr. Maloney had just turned forty. Statistically speaking, he was on the second half of his life span. It was time to decide what he was going to be when he grew up.

The college called him for the interview on a Thursday evening, while he was Googling career choices on the Internet. He got the e-mail the morning after the interview, while his students were at counseling class. "Your 101 class will be using *Introduction to Elementary Science*," the e-mail read. "You can pick up the teacher's edition at the college book-store."

A transformed Mr. Maloney gathered up his youngsters from counseling class.

They had asked him all of the right questions at the interview . . . and none of the wrong ones. When the committee had asked him about his philosophy of education, he had told them the truth. He believed every child was like a tulip bulb in spring, waiting to unfold. He believed the classroom should be a child's paradise, with "hands-on" learning at every turn. He believed his investment in the life of a child would reap dividends for society in years to come. He believed teaching was a great privilege and a sobering responsibility. He believed a teacher should live learning, breathe learning, embrace learning.

The committee had not asked him if he managed to achieve this goal, only if that was what he believed. They had asked all the right questions at the interview.

Energized by a fresh start, Mr. Maloney prepared an opening session that would hold the attention of even a young adult in the information age—it could compete with cell phones, texting, and iPods. Dressed in a suit and tie, he handed his impressive agenda, along with a boiled egg, a bottle, and a match, to the students as they entered the classroom. As he demonstrated for his future teachers that fire needs oxygen to keep going (thus when deprived creating pressure and sucking the egg through the bottle), no one was texting. (Next week, he would make a volcano.)

As he watched his college students light their matches, Mr. Maloney remembered the time little Eugene Pelfry had accidentally caused a small explosion during the chemistry experiment. The alarm was ringing, classes were clearing the building, and the fire department was on its way within minutes. He remembered how dry his mouth went and the way his heart was hammering as he explained the accident to the principal, Mr. Pearson. There was nothing dull about Mr. Maloney's third grade science class back then.

His colleagues' sons and daughters had always ended up on his roster somehow in those early years. But this year, three faculty members' children had been up for third grade. They all ended up in Mrs. Stolte's class.

"I tried to get Junior put in your class," Mr. Howard had assured him under his breath at the staff luncheon last fall, "but I guess Mr. Pearson forgot."

Mr. Maloney appreciated the sensitive gesture, but he knew in his heart it was a lie. Teachers knew when other teachers had hit the wall. Nobody knew better than his colleagues.

Between his Monday night class and his Thursday night class, Mr. Maloney checked on teacher retirement. He had a few years to go, but he could always buy some years.

Mr. Maloney liked the way his college students hushed when he came in the room. He liked being able to complete a sentence without an interruption. He liked leaving his class feeling as fresh and alert as he had been when he entered, not with his nerves frayed, his brain fried, and his name over-used. "Mr. Maloney, hey, Mr. Maloney, over here, Mr. Maloney. . . ."

This was the same year as the elementary school lockdown. As Mr. Maloney sweated away the twenty-minute wait sandwiched between ten giddy girls and twelve perspiring boys in the classroom restroom, he began to realize that this was not just another drill. This was the real McCoy.

At last, Mr. Pearson's voice came over the intercom. "Teachers, this is not a drill. Please continue your lockdown procedures."

"Mr. Maloney, I have to go to the bathroom," whispered Maggie Maye.

Mr. Maloney had always loved cops and robbers. Under different circumstances, he might have tolerated things well. A car theft half a mile from the school, the high-speed police chase, the stolen car crashing into the mayor's picket fence across the street, blaring sirens, flashing, blue lights. . . . If the truth be told, he had always been partial to adrenaline-pumping events. But Maggie Maye had to go to the bathroom.

The next day, Mr. Maloney called Teachers' Retirement to see how much it would cost to buy out his remaining years.

He liked teaching adults. They were . . . less needy. He had often wondered what it would be like to go into a quiet office on a Monday morning and have a cup of coffee, instead of a classroom where children were waiting, like a swarm of flies, to descend on him.

After the volcano, his 101 class studied electricity, the solar system, and insects. Insects were his favorite.

"I wish all college classes were like this," said one of Mr. Maloney's freshmen. "I bet your third graders can't wait to get to school."

Mr. Maloney remembered himself, fifteen years younger and thirty pounds lighter, carrying his famous aquarium into the elementary school building. It was just a simple, ten-gallon rectangular tank, but it played various roles throughout the year. In the fall, it housed Monarch habitats. In the spring, tadpoles developed between its transparent walls. In between, he brought in hermit crabs, and sometimes furry rodents.

"Whatcha got this time, Mr. Maloney?" kids from all grades would ask as they gathered around him, peering into his versatile habitat. It was not uncommon in those days for a group of curious children to escort Mr. Maloney all the way to his classroom on the east wing, or for one to pop in occasionally in the school day on their way to the bathroom. "Hey, Mr. Maloney, uh, I was just wonderin' . . . got anything new at the science center?"

What had happened to Mr. Maloney, the science teacher? Was it the endless paperwork or all those committee meetings? The deadbeat bus duties (you stand in front of a gym full of four hundred bored children for forty-five minutes, and expect them not to act up). Or was it the repeated phone calls to the guidance counselor, the truancy officer, and the social workers? Somewhere between test scores and data analyzing, custody battles and behavior disorder referrals, portfolios and scripted instruction, his pleasure in teaching had faded away.

Crowd control—that was what his life amounted to—holding back the masses. Too many hands, all reaching for him to save them, as the storm raged relentlessly around their little ship. There weren't enough lifeboats. How could he choose? Helpless, hating himself, he watched the waves take the ship under.

This was why he did not like Monday mornings. This was why he was moonlighting.

He was careful not to share too much of the negative stuff with his future teachers in his college class. Why burst their bubble now? Reality would set in way too soon anyway.

Instead, he filled the empty gaps in his frustrated life with late-night hours planning his 101 agenda, researching on the Internet, and rounding up materials to illustrate a science center to die for.

The best science centers had some living things in them. He was convinced of that.

Mr. Maloney recalled the year the baby guinea pigs were born. He had left his classroom after dismissal the afternoon before, the mother looking like a little, round balloon. When he returned the following morning, three baby guinea pigs were nestled together, nursing their mommy. "And I have one more item," Mr. Pearson had said over the intercom later that day, to wrap up his afternoon announcements. "Mr. Maloney's class proudly announces the births of their guinea pigs—

Winken, Blinken, and Nod—who together weighed in at a whopping 11 and a half ounces. Please keep visits short, so the little family can bond."

"Are you going straight home, Mr. Maloney?" asked one of his college freshmen as they walked him to his car after class.

"No, I've got an errand to run," said Mr. Maloney. "I need to stop by the pet store."

The wave of excitement in the elementary school lobby as Mr. Maloney brought in the long, awkward tub the next morning rippled into the hallway where he made his way through with his guinea pigs.

"Can I hold one, Mr. Maloney?"

"What are they?"

"What do you feed them, Mr. Maloney?"

"Meet me at recess. You can help me pull grass," Mr. Maloney replied.

On the last night of the college semester, Mr. Maloney changed the quick-write format. He asked the students to tell what they had learned from this class that they could take with them.

As the students were finishing up, he picked up Mrs. Cordle's quick-write.

Dear Mr. Maloney,

There is not enough time to say all the things I want to say. So, I will just name a few. It had been a quarter of a century since I had stepped into a college classroom. I came into your room a little nervous. Would I measure up? Could I keep up with these bright, young minds?

There you were, with that egg-in-a-bottle experiment. You made us laugh, and you put me at ease the first meeting.

As you have demonstrated for us the heart of a true teacher, it has become my goal to be the best teacher that ever walked into a classroom. I want my students to want to be there.

When you brought in your "critters," told us jokes, taught us little songs (my personal favorite was, "I'm Being Swallowed By A Boa Constrictor"), and read us little stories (I loved that true story about the baby whale rescue, by the way), I could see that you are exactly where you belong. How blessed the children must be who walk through your classroom door. The parents must hope their children get in Mr. Maloney's room.

Well, I've got a few years on you, Mr. Maloney. But I just wanted to say, "When I grow up, I want to be just like you."

Mr. Maloney tucked the quick-write into his pocket.

A handful of students lingered around his desk. "Bye, Mr. Maloney," smiled Paulette.

"Thanks. I enjoyed the semester," added Jacob.

"Well, have a good summer, Mr. Maloney," said Jessica. "How many years until you get to retire?"

"Retire? Oh, I don't know," sighed Mr. Maloney, looking up at her over his reading glasses. "They may not get rid of me for a long time yet." He leaned back in his chair. "They may have to carry me out on a stretcher."

(They had asked him all the right questions at the interview.)

THROUGH HIS EYES

Mr. Pearson hung up the phone, and sank back in his TV chair. One of the finest men he had ever known had passed away. As he drove to Mr. Maloney's home to be with the family and staff who were gathering there, his mind raced to a conversation the two men had had just weeks earlier.

"Ever think about giving it up, Jack?"

"Yes, especially on dark winter mornings when it's so cold outside and my body can't wake up as quickly as it used to. How about you, Wendell?"

"Oh, lots of times. But then a former student will run into me at the grocery store, or one of my own grandkids will let me know how much they admire that I'm a teacher, and I change my mind. I guess I'm just too much of an old softie, Jack. I love being in a school. I love being in a classroom with inquiring minds—so full of potential, and so in need of a good, practical science lesson. This gets addictive doesn't it?"

"What, caring for people? Loving and helping kids? Being a mentor? Being a good role model? Yep, I guess it does, Wendell . . . I guess it does."

"Well, I tell you what I'm planning, Jack. I'm going to teach two more years, and then I'm going to retire and take Millie on that cruise I've been promising her. So, you mark it down. Two years."

"Only if you'll promise to come back and sponsor our science club."

"You've got a deal, Mr. Pearson. You've got a deal."

"Oh, Wendell, before you leave . . . I wanted to share this letter with you that I received from the college the other day. You deserve to see what they think of you. I must say, I think they're so high on you and how their students rave about your teaching, they'd hire you away from me in a heartbeat. You know, as much as we'd miss you around here, if you really want to move on to higher ed full-time, I'd certainly support your decision."

"Two years, Jack. In two years, I'm going to take you up on that. I'd be there tomorrow with bells on, 'cause I absolutely love working with the college age group; reminds me of the spark I had when I was a rookie just starting out. When I'm in front of those young minds, many of them now teachers themselves, it's as if I'm born again. But, we're raising one of our grandsons, and he's halfway through college. I can't let him down when he's this close to finishing. In two years, I can afford it, . . . Just two years . . ."

As Mr. Pearson pulled into the driveway of his colleague and dear friend, Mr. Maloney's wife met him in the yard and asked him if he would speak at the funeral.

"It would mean so much to him, Jack. He absolutely thought the world of you."

"Yes, I will, and I am honored to be asked, Helen. One of the finest men I've ever known."

"You know, Jack, I found a brochure he had put back. He was going to take me on a cruise. But I didn't need a cruise. Living every day with this good, good man was all I ever needed."

"He made our school a special place to be. His science lab was the best. But more than that, he was such a role model to the kids. Oh, they will miss him so. Our staff will miss him so. The entire community will miss him so . . . Tell me, Helen, why did he go into teaching? When you all were in college, do you remember how he made that decision?"

"I will never forget it. We were standing on the steps of the library one night, talking about our future. He had been offered a huge scholarship to go on to grad school to study engineering. Wendell just looked me in the eyes, and said, 'I need to give back. We need more people who understand that concept. It's not about me, Helen. It's about others. As a teacher, I can do that every day. So, that's what I'm going to do.'"

"And at our school, Helen, he did give—every day."

Mr. Pearson slowly walked into the home of his dear friend, Mr. Maloney—realizing that in two years, most likely, Wendell would not really have retired after all.

REFLECTIONS

1. Does your school district have any type of "relief" process or sup-
    port system for teachers who are hitting the wall, but who can't yet
    retire?
2. What do you think attributes to early burnout in a teacher's career?
3. Why do students love teachers who bring a lot of variety and "real-
    world" experiences to the classroom? Why then don't we do more
    of this?

SOLUTIONS

In *The Truth About Burnout* (Maslach and Leiter 1997), the authors address
the reality that organizations are often the cause of personal stress in the
work place. The university realized years ago that if it wanted professors
to stay on the cutting edge, they would need a period of "renewal" peri-
odically throughout their career. Hence, the sabbatical was born.

But for some reason, in pre-K–12, apparently due to summer breaks,
this has not been a strategy that has been seriously pursued in most
states, and the teaching profession has suffered as a result.

The fact that there are dozens of articles and websites available that
address teacher burnout attest to the fact that stress and burnout are a
common problem. Some of the stressors cited are lack of parental support, and pressure from higher up to perform non-teaching tasks, as in
rubrics, curriculum mapping, and reports (Greenberg, 2011). Add to that
the unique stressors for teachers of very young children, and the fact that
the social–emotional domain they patiently develop in their young is not
measured or applauded by the academic community on the high-stakes
standardized tests (though without it, children would be unable to function as productive students or citizens).

In its volume 3, issue 1 publication, the editorial staff of *Teaching
Young Children* outlines ten strategies for teachers to combat burnout in
the early childhood classroom. These include networking, cultivating a
hobby, and the basics of good health—sleep, nutrition, and exercise—as
well as prioritizing, making time for self, practicing relaxation (such as
journal writing), and taking time to get inspired.

But is this enough? Classroom teachers, band directors, coaches—anyone who works with and supervises kids day after day for nine and a half

months out of the year—need some type of built-in buffer for personal growth and renewal at regular intervals throughout their career.

The sabbatical essential would not only extend careers, but would benefit students greatly, as fewer teachers would hit the wall long before retirement age (i.e., those who feel they have no choice but to keep teaching until retirement).

Also, the benefits to the body of knowledge in the various disciplines would be significant, as teachers would be visiting other schools, reading, traveling, providing training, researching, and sharpening the saw—much like their colleagues in higher education.

And perhaps yearlong breaks in classroom service are not necessarily the answer. Perhaps more frequent, shorter intervals of a few weeks are a more practical, smarter way to go. Substitute teachers could be trained and ready to step in while the resident teacher is away, and the sabbatical could result in reporting findings and training of the faculty upon return.

California is one state that has stepped into the waters. *The Survive and Thrive Mini-Sabbatical Intervention Program* is sponsored by the California Teachers Association and conducted by Dr. Byron Greenberg. In this life-changing five days, the areas of time-management, stress-management, nutrition, and relationship-building are addressed. Follow-up continues at regular intervals after the event.

If other states follow suit and extend these rescue retreats to include opportunities for research, the schools could soon be rich with fresh perspectives, ongoing professional development, and a research arm that has been hugely missed over the years.

The call for educators to be better trained and more respected by our society is perhaps louder today than ever before. When we learn to not work our teachers as if they are on an assembly line, and learn more about their mental, emotional, physical, and intellectual needs due to the stressors of their work, we just may see a transformational change take place in the classroom—for students, and also their mentors.

SIX

Miss Teacher

(If This Toddler Could Talk)

NAEYC STANDARD 1: PROMOTING CHILD DEVELOPMENT AND
LEARNING

*1a: Knowing and Understanding Young Children's Characteristics and Needs,
from Birth through Age 8*

Dear Miss Teacher,

My name is Chasity, and I need you. I have been taken from my mommy
three times now. Then my new mommy brought me here. At first, I
thought this place was another family. Another home. Another not-forever. But my new mommy came back. Every day, she comes back. So this
is my home in the daytime and that is my home at night.

That might be okay.`

If . . .

If I can learn how to tell you what I need. Nobody taught me words
and everything sounds so muffled in my ears. Little kids half my size
have lots of words. Big words. And here I am, this big-for-my-age tot
who can't talk. It makes me mad when they can't hear me. So I bite. Or
hit. Or pull hair.

It's okay for you to stop me. Please stop me. But while you're doing
that, let me know that I'm not bad; that I count. I used to cry for hours in
my crib with the pain in my ears. Sometimes, nobody came. So I learned

to cry shrill. My shrill cry means, "Somebody hear me. Somebody help me. Somebody tell me I'm somebody."

They like me at the new house. They feed me every time I'm hungry. They bathe me every day. They sit in the floor and play with me. ME! I'm warm, always warm when it's cold outside. They bring me medicine when my ears hurt. I am rocked; rocked back and forth in a chair while my new mommy sings to me. I sing with her, loud words that nobody can understand because I don't have words yet. Before, except in the not-forever homes, I always rocked myself. Back and forth in my bed I rock; until the pain goes away from my ears; until I fall asleep.

Please rock me, too, Miss Teacher. My daytime mommy.

I try. I try really hard to talk to the boys and girls. I have almost never been around other children. I get so excited! Little people the size of me! They're more interesting than toys! I want to play with them. I want to touch them and make them talk to me. They turn away. They run away. So I bite. Or hit. Or pull hair. Help me, please help me Miss Teacher, to learn to enter their groups.

While I'm here, give me something to do. I'm much smarter than people think, and I get bored. (So I bite. Or hit. Or pull hair.) Give me something to do that fills up my mind. So long, too long, there was gray and silence. Nobody talked to me or showed me things. I love to make things happen: the way the paint puts a color on the paper and it stays; bright colors, loud colors, forever colors.

I can't get enough of the puzzles, Miss Teacher. The way everything fits together like it should. There was no order in my topsy-turvy world. The puzzles are like this room, Miss Teacher. First, the centers, next meal time, then nap. Every day, I can count on it. My world stops spiraling out of control.

I am musical. Some people don't know what to make of it because I rock back and forth—sway wide left and right—to the music. Don't they know I'm feeling it? The music feels so good. Maybe I'm gifted. Maybe underneath these developmental delays, there's a miracle waiting to happen. Maybe that's why I dance in the aisles in my new family's church. Maybe that's why I grabbed the hands of the offering man and danced to the piano song. He smiled. Everybody smiled. And you are smiling, too. Keep smiling, Miss Teacher. Tell me I'm somebody. Tell me I'm good.

It is time to go home, Miss Teacher. There she is standing in the door just like yesterday and the day before: my new mommy. My forever mommy? She holds her arms out wide. I run to her. I am scooped up in her arms and she delights in me.

I have never been delighted in before, Miss Teacher. Tomorrow, I will come back. Soon, I will start crying after my new (forever?) mommy. Please don't be offended. This is the first attachment I have ever formed. Please take me in your arms and comfort me. Tell me Mommy will be back. Tell me she loves me, and you love me, too. Sing me a song. I will sing loud words you don't understand. I will dance and sway far to the left and far to the right. Smile and delight in me. Take me to the story books and show me the pictures. There is so much to see, so much to know, so much lost time to make up for. Then we will go to the art center and paint. Please paint a picture of my new family. Paint my new daddy, big and safe, his arm around my mommy. Paint my new brothers in their rough and tumble play. Paint my new big sisters, tall and kind and beautiful. And there, in the middle, paint me. Bright colors. Happy colors. Forever colors.

THROUGH HIS EYES

A classmate had posted the writing in an online assignment. (Mr. Pearson had at last been able to carve out enough time to begin his doctorate, and he had the privilege of sharing the discussion board with fellow educators who worked with a wide range of ages in children.)

Students from his school immediately came to mind, and Mr. Pearson had to blink back tears. But it was Mrs. Carwall's face that he kept seeing. Mr. Pearson had always wondered how she did it, how any of the teachers of his youngest children stayed in the job day after day, year after year.

The needs were so great, and so many—the younger the children, the needier they were. How very ironic then, that the workers in the infants and toddlers daycare down the street were paid far less than the teachers of any other age group (and they had no benefits and minimal sick days).

Mr. Pearson had always feared that when he had to come in Mrs. Carwall's classroom to deliver a message or to conference with her briefly, he would be asked to substitute while she took care of business. Mr. Pearson loved his children, and he treasured spending time with them, but he couldn't imagine spending a day taking care of twenty of their kind, and with only one other adult in the room to help him—or thirty minutes for that matter. He would, he was sure, lose his mind.

So it was with sincerity that he replied to his classmate's post.

Marlene,

I'm a principal in an elementary school, and I have always had a deep admiration for the teachers of the very small children. Can you list the things I might do to make their day less stressful, things that might free them up to spend more productive time with their children?

Hats off to you,
Jack

The list came the same day he posted:

Jack,

Thanks for your understanding. If my director were to ask me such a question, these are the things I would list:

Please give me some down time. I love my little ones so very much, and they need all of me. I cannot go full-force ahead for several consecutive hours if I haven't taken the time to breathe deep or go to the bathroom, or phone home and make sure my own sick child is okay.

Please give me respect. Don't assume that because I teach the little ones, I am not as smart as a college professor. I may be much smarter. I know how to juggle many things and to multitask like no other, and I understand child development and all of the ages and stages. I have the emotional intelligence to know when it's time to walk away, but I have the passion for children to know I'll be coming back. I can communicate with someone who has no words, and I can have a positive relationship with a group of little people who are totally egocentric.

Please don't think that my groceries don't cost as much as yours. It costs as much to fill up my tank with gas as it does yours. I, like you, have kids to feed, and some day, I want to send them to college. Pay me what I'm worth.

Please don't put on that distant face when I tell you I'm concerned about a child's home life. I'm supposed to report this to the authorities—I'm keeping the law, not breaking it—so please don't give me that look like I'm causing trouble (again).

Last, please provide training for me that is useful. 20% of my babies are in grandparent or foster care, 25% have parents who are incarcerated, a staggering number were born addicted, and close to half have been touched by substance abuse. I need help. I need to know what to expect and how to manage it.

That's what your early childhood teachers need from you, Jack.

Thanks for asking,
Marlene

REFLECTIONS

1. How does your school prepare its teachers for the cultural problems impacting our children's lives and development?
2. Are the teachers of different grade levels in your school provided opportunities to team up before the new school year in order to work toward a seamless transition for children?
3. What implications do early childhood teachers' lower salaries have that might impact value and morale?

SOLUTIONS

According to the Child Welfare Information Gateway, nearly four hundred thousand children were in foster care in 2012. With the explosion of drug abuse, especially of methamphetamine, the need for foster care has increased dramatically. (Experts estimate that 80 to 90 percent of placements can be traced to drug abuse.) Research has found that traumatized children's brains develop differently. Though their IQs may be normal or high, they tend to be developmentally below their chronological age due to the impact of trauma. (For example, a four-year-old may respond to frustration like a two-year-old, or a middle schooler may behave like an elementary student.) Therefore, the need for teacher training on managing the behaviors and needs of traumatized children is upon us. These children are not going to just be able to "snap out of it" the day (or year) they are placed in a (hopefully) safe home . . . again. . . .

We have come a long way in recognizing the need for early intervention. The fact that the federal and state governments are funneling millions of dollars into early childhood education testifies that there is vast

potential in it. Significant funds are invested in early intervention programs that target at-risk children as early as birth. Furthermore, there are
excellent scholarship programs in place to get early childhood teachers
trained and certified. For example, the KIDS NOW scholarship in Kentucky will pay up to $1,800 per year toward a college student's tuition in
early childhood all the way through the bachelor's program if the student
is employed twenty hours or more per week in an early childhood program that qualifies and participates.

However, we still have a long way to go in raising the status of early
childhood teachers and workers. Though children in the first three years
of life are in the critical "formative years," their caregivers, on average,
are the lowest-paid teachers on the scale. Not only do we need to keep
clearing the roadblocks for early childhood workers to get their BA, but
we need to see the salaries of teachers and instructional assistants with
their associate's degree raised to a level that reflects their education . . .
and their worth.

SEVEN

Mrs. Carwall's Student

Blessed are they that mourn: for they shall be comforted.

—Matthew 5:4

STANDARD 7: EARLY CHILDHOOD FIELD EXPERIENCES

7b. Opportunities to Observe and Practice in at Least Two of the Three Main Types of Early Education Settings (Early School Grades, Child Care Centers and Homes, Head Start Programs)

NAEYC STANDARD 5: USING CONTENT KNOWLEDGE TO BUILD MEANINGFUL CURRICULUM

5a: Understanding Content Knowledge and Resources in Academic Disciplines: Language and Literacy; the Arts—Music, Creative Movement, Dance, Drama, Visual Arts; Mathematics; Science, Physical Activity, Physical Education, Health and Safety; and Social Studies

He didn't have a name or any kind of pull. Heck, he didn't even have a toothbrush. Or a ball. He had knowledge—not of things any child should ever know.

As an infant, he was failing to thrive until they took him out of the home. Somebody somewhere—he didn't know who—must have loved him somehow, for he had survived. Then they put him back in his home; his personal hell.

By the time he went to school, Homer had given up again. There was no light in his eyes. No sign of curiosity. And he barely ever talked.

That was the year (and it had to be the Equalizer who stepped in, for he had no one to pull strings for him), that was the year things evened out a bit. He was put in Mrs. Carwall's class.

It wasn't that Mrs. Carwall was perfect. Having survived a difficult childhood herself, Mrs. Carwall had some rough edges. She was suspicious of other adults, and her knee-jerk reaction to any perceived insult was verbal aggression. However, on the flip side, the same difficult childhood had left Mrs. Carwall fiercely determined to protect children and unusually perceptive to those suffering as she had suffered. Mrs. Carwall didn't like teaching—she loved it. It was her passion, her calling, her hobby, her art.

Walking into her classroom was one and the same with walking into a child's paradise. Children felt accepted as soon as they entered. It was almost a temptation to leave your shoes at the door . . . for this was indeed "holy ground." As much as some of her colleagues disliked her, they all respected her.

Though consisting of three- and four-year-olds, the classroom was anything but chaotic. The children moved around the room with remarkable self-control. They knew the rules, and for the most part, observed them. Every freedom had a qualifier. They could choose any activity they wished, *but* they must finish it before starting a new one. They could engage with anybody in the room at any time, *but* all interactions must be positive, and they were all friends. It was a safe place for a boy like Homer.

For a child raised in a colorless world, the room was full of beauty and order and light. But for a child raised in overstimulation, the environment was balanced, with an attractive mix of neutral colors and bolder ones. It was a colorful place for a boy like Homer.

Each new activity was introduced and then left on an open shelf for exploration. When completed, it was put back on its tray as the teacher modeled the words, "I stand up, I push my chair in, I put my things away." It was a predictable place for a boy like Homer. (By Christmas, he had smiled once.)

Homer's teacher cared about the whole child. Each day, Mrs. Carwall made sure all of her children got an adequate amount of time to develop their gross motor skills, and if weather permitted, this took place out in the fresh air.

Homer's teacher cared about the whole child. The birthday parties were not filled with sweets and chips, but fruity snacks, yogurt, and finger sandwiches. And though an avid supporter of PTA, Mrs. Carwall dared them to bring the sugary, salty snacks to the classroom and sell them to the more privileged children to eat in front of the other kids (yes, a tradition that has somehow escaped scrutiny in our schools).

Mrs. Carwall was once approached about this by the guidance counselor. "You're breaking school policy," she was told.

"Now, Billie Jo," replied Mrs. Carwall. "Our school really doesn't want to air this piece of dirty laundry on the six o'clock news. Do we?" No one ever approached her about it again.

Homer's teacher cared about the whole child. At the well-stocked art center, Homer was free to create anything he pleased. It was always accepted, and never compared to others. Not once did Homer's snowman fail to make the team of identical snowmen on the bulletin board, because there were no identical snowmen. Instead, there was a vast array of glorious creations from the hearts and hands of preschoolers, no two alike, and none ever altered in any way by "professional" hands.

Mrs. Carwall and her team guarded Homer's heart like a pack of watchdogs. If a classmate made a remark about his speech delay, Mrs. Carwall would intervene with skill, "Homer has a lot to say, just give him time. Homer, would you like to build a tower with Caleb here? I'll help."

Habitually proactive, Mrs. Carwall would arrange for older student mentors or community volunteers to be stand-in parents for the "Homers" in her room at the classroom parties, field trips, and school performances. She made the matches at the beginning of the year so that the same shepherd could be assigned to the child consistently throughout the year.

Mrs. Carwall cared about the whole child. Her reading corner was filled with storybooks that addressed the worlds of children from all experiences, including children in poverty and children in fear. Mrs. Carwall's reading corner validated the fact that not all children grow up in a suburban home with two smiling parents, a happy brother and sister, and a friendly dog named Flip. (Heck, the only dogs in Homer's life were kept starving and mean for fighting entertainment.) The reading corner was a comforting place.

Mrs. Carwall's year wasn't the year Homer was delivered from his personal hell (though it *was* the year the light came back into his eyes). But Mrs. Carwall was one in a long line of concerned citizens who made that phone call. (In fact, she made six. Not to mention the traditional two home visits, with not her aide this time, but Mr. Pearson serving as her bodyguard.)

The first phone call took place the evening she ran into Homer in the grocery store. His mom's boyfriend was cussing him out. Mrs. Carwall marched straight up to the pair—the articulate words were already in her mouth to line the monster out—when Homer looked up and caught her eye. His blackened eyes begged her not to recognize him. Trembling with emotion, she hesitated for an eternal moment, and then walked away.

Before nightfall, social services were at Homer's door. (By the third grade, they would deliver him. Permanently. He would end up in the home of the family he couldn't remember—the ones who had loved him as an infant and who had given him back his will to live. Homer would be safe at last, and loved.)

But that was four long years away. In the meantime, Homer was given a year of respite by the Equalizer: ten months of mornings he couldn't wait to get out of bed; ten months of unconditional positive regard; something new every day; fairy tales and puppet shows; sidewalk chalk rainbows on the playground; and fly-trapping plants at the discovery center. He had long, uninterrupted periods of sunshine and fresh air as his teacher dared the standardized test worshipers to take their recess away, protected interactions with other children as he slowly learned to talk, and magical moments curled up beside his teacher in the rocking chair as she read to him about the wonders of the animal kingdom.

Homer didn't live in a nice suburban home with two smiling parents, and neither he nor his siblings had a big name (or a nice dog).

But he was somebody now. He was Mrs. Carwall's student.

(And in case it's not yet clear whose son Homer was destined to be, she made six calls for him his preschool year, and she had given him back his will to live—twice.)

THROUGH HIS EYES

Mr. Pearson breathed a long sigh of relief. He and his staff had worried for years about this little boy. They had done everything they knew to do to get Homer in a safe situation. Now, at last, Homer was in a loving home—for good—and with one of the team. How much sense that made! Once, when he was younger and gutsier, Mr. Pearson had read that blood-curdling novel by Dave Pelzer, *A Child Called "It."* He had loathed the school staff in the story for letting outrageous abuse go on under their noses for many years before the young victim was at last rescued. He had made up his mind then and there that would never happen on his watch.

Easier said than done. But at last, another child had been safely pulled to shore. He and his team could sleep well tonight. Until the next time. . . .

REFLECTIONS

1. What practices does your school have that may put financial pressure on low-income families?
2. Does your administration encourage feedback from teachers about the policies they may not embrace?
3. What are the components of your school that would make it a haven for a child in a hellish situation?

SOLUTIONS

In a documented case from the 1960s in New York, a young woman was stabbed and murdered on a public street while a crowd of thirty-eight passersby failed to intervene. Psychology's term for this incredibly deplorable case of group paralysis is the bystander effect. Unfortunately, many other horrific crimes with the same disturbing lack of response from onlookers have since been documented both in our nation and worldwide. Research explains that people are often "inhibited by a complex web of social pressures and group norms, especially in crowds" (Ray B. Williams, *Psychology Today*, October 24, 2011).

Similar crimes happen to children every day behind closed doors, and adults who know in their hearts that it is happening fail to report.

Why?

There are many reasons: fear of retaliation; fear the report will back-fire on the child; lack of sufficient evidence; the belief that we're stepping over our boundaries, and that someone else will take care of it; indifference; ignorance; and many more.

Here are the facts: All states require teachers and school personnel to report suspected child abuse. Many states require any person to report. Usually a reasonable suspicion, or a reasonable cause to believe, is enough to require a teacher to report according to the law. As a rule, when in doubt, report. Reporting is anonymous, and an investigation will take place. Failure to report can result in a criminal or civil liability.

Every state has a hotline number for reporting suspected child abuse. The national child abuse hotline number is 1-800-4-A-Child.

Though social consciousness has been raised concerning the "white, middle-class" curriculums and assessments we once used with the masses, we are still guilty of middle-class practices in our schools. While the tradition of using children to raise money for their school is widely accepted because the students do need and benefit from the items and services their schools purchase from these funds, schools sometimes cross over the line from benefiting children to exploiting them.

It is absolutely unacceptable to sell food in our classrooms to children in front of other children of lower income homes and let the first group eat while the latter group watches. Not only are we being insensitive to the children's (and their parents') feelings, but we are feeding (literally) the national childhood obesity epidemic by bringing still more sugary, fatty, and salty snacks into the children's daily diet. (What often happens is that the teachers feel obligated to feed the remainder of the class, which can run into a significant amount of out-of-pocket expense in a year's time.)

This is just one example. What about the long school supply lists that are being required of parents at the beginning of each school year? Though this practice, like many others, started out small and reasonable, it has, in some districts, lost all sense of balance. It is not unheard of now for a child to bring home a seventy-five dollar (or more) school supply list. Multiply that child by three or four siblings and the parent has to come up with a few hundred dollars besides the back-to-school clothing expenses.

Not only are we drawing a visible line between the rich and the poor children in our schools, but we are alienating parents, and that is never a good thing. The last thing a struggling family needs is more pressure. That may put a few more dry-erase markers in the stockpile, but it won't help our school in the long run.

In bringing the community on board, schools could raise funds. We want big businesses in the community to donate? Take the children out into the community, and make the citizens proud of what we're doing. (Don't expect the citizens to come to our shows. Go to them. The city park. The community center. Local churches or country clubs.) Feature our clogging team. Put on a wonderful production of *The Sound of Music*. Blast them with a talent show. Build camaraderie, and then invite the merchants to dig into their pockets. We might take in more in one show than in a whole year of feeding junk food to obese children (while hungry children watch). And we could have a community gloating over their young prodigies, instead of resenting the money drain.

EIGHT

Ratios

*5c: Using Own Knowledge, Appropriate Early Learning Standards, and Other
Resources to Design, Implement, and Evaluate Developmentally Meaningful
and Challenging Curriculum for Each Child*

It was only 9:45 a.m., and Ms. Tracy had almost completed a thought.
It was something about ratios. Nothing about her morning had been out
of the ordinary.

At 8:00, her little crew had arrived with stories to tell and needs to be
met. "Miss Tracy, that boy in Miss Peterson's class stole my reading book
right out of my backpack!"

"Hey, Miss Tracy, I caught a grasshopper this morning. Can we keep
him?"

The phone began to ring just as McKayla's dad was explaining that
McKayla got hold of the scissors over the weekend and cut her own
bangs. Ms. Tracy glanced at McKayla's bangless, little forehead, and
smiled to Mr. McKinley as she picked up the phone, "My little sister did
the same thing when we were children. . . . Hello. This is Ms. Tracy," she
said into the phone.

McKayla's dad laughed, comforted. "McKayla, you're beautiful," he
heard his daughter's teacher say reassuringly as he left the room, just
before the tardy bell rang. "Good-bye, Mr. McKinley. Have a nice day,"
Ms. Tracy called.

"Yes, Michael just got here," she answered into the phone. "Could I wait until the building clears?" (She didn't like to send children out of the classroom while parents were still in the building. You just couldn't be too careful these days. Even after the parents were gone, if she sent a child on an errand, she sent a partner, too.)

Another little fellow tugged at her arm. "Just a minute, Tommy. I'm on the phone."

Mei Ling's mother stopped in to see if it would be all right to bring treats for her birthday today. "Absolutely. Any time after 2:00 would be just perfect."

Ms. Tracy headed toward the metal cabinet, while it was on her mind, to fish out the birthday crown. On her way to the cabinet, she asked Scotty if he had eaten breakfast this morning, found him a snack and the hand sanitizer, and submitted the attendance on the computer while reminding the children to hang up their backpacks and put their folders in their cubbies. (She never made it to the metal cabinet.)

Ethan came in late (again), and when Ethan came in late, it was never a quiet affair. He burst into the classroom, enthusiastically calling, "I'm here, Ms. Tracy!"

"Good morning, Ethan dear, but please don't forget your inside voice. Hang up your backpack, and let's get started on your bell work. (Have you had your breakfast?)"

After the pledge to the flag, Ms. Tracy picked up her reading manual and felt her heart skip just a little. Even now, after all these years, there was still joy in teaching little people to read. She herded her littlest flock to the reading table and rubbed her hands together. Now, to get down to the business of teaching.

On the way to the table, there had been only three or four interruptions. Ms. Tracy reminded Chloe not to run with scissors, and Dennis asked her to tie his shoe. She asked him where his reading book was; he said it was in his backpack. She asked him to get it out. He said his backpack was in the car. She stooped to tie his shoe, and her classroom telephone rang.

The secretary asked if she would send Dennis (or was it Dalton? No, it had to be Dennis) to the office to pick up his backpack. His mother had dropped it off.

"Yes, as soon as I tie his shoe."

Ms. Tracy reached the reading table. By now, it looked like an oasis in a desert. She could have kissed the ground it stood on. "Who remembers the story for today?"

Her classroom door flew open. "Ms. Tracy, did you forget this is Book Fair Week?"

"Book Fair Week? Quiet!" she added instinctively, just before the excited murmur began to ripple through her room. She glanced at the clock: three reading groups to squeeze in before lunch.

"Quiet, children. Line leaders, push your chairs in and line up. Do not run. Do *not* run. Fifth block from the door. Leave plenty of room to open the door."

A tug on her sleeve and a wail from across the room. "Somebody stole my book fair money!"

Ms. Tracy reassured, "I've got it here, Cassie. It's in the Book Fair tub."

Little people crowded around her, reaching for their money. "Patient, step back. I will read your name on your baggie. Boys, push your chairs in and *walk* to the door. I said *walk* to the door.

"Scottie, please push in your chair. . . . Never mind—Mei Ling got it. Thank you, Mei Ling, for being a good neighbor. Remind me when we get back to get your birthday crown."

Again, a tug on her sleeve.

"Yes, Amy?"

"May I go to Mommy's room and get my money?"

Ms. Tracy nodded. "We'll meet you in the library, Amy. . . . Would you go with her, Mei Ling? You can be my helper today since you're the birthday girl. Girls, push in your chairs and walk quietly to the door. Cassie, please go back to your seat. We don't run in the room. Fifth block from the door, boys. Please don't crowd the door."

Ms. Tracy switched off the lights and opened the door. "Pedro, please make sure nobody's in the bathroom. Cassie, line up at the end of the line."

Central office had told the teachers last year they couldn't write "stress" on their sick cards any more. It was not excusable. At the bottom of the sick card, the teacher had to sign under the words, "I solemnly swear that I could not perform my duties. . . ."

After a long stretch of days like this one, it was never a problem to solemnly swear, because it was always true by then. The problem was what to put on the line above, where it said "nature of illness."

Since they were not supposed to write "stress," Ms. Tracy had considered writing "insanity prevention," but she was not sure how that would go over.

So she went through her list of personal, chronic problems, and tried hopefully to remember if any of them had flared up lately. She could honestly say she had allergies. She could honestly say she had low iron.

She was trying hard to be fair, so she went on down the list. She could honestly say she had heart palpitations. She could honestly say she had gastrointestinal issues—just not lately.

She could honestly say she had cycles. She could honestly say she had biorhythms. Her spirits began to lift. There just might be a connection here.

The clamor around her in the library brought Ms. Tracy back to the here and now and the book fair madness. "Miss Tracy, how much money is two quarters and four nickels? Can I buy that cool poster with this much?"

"Honey, you need two dollars to buy this, maybe tomorrow."

And then the dreaded sticky finger episode. "Ms. Tracy," whispered one of the parent volunteers, "I saw Cassie put a sparkly pencil in her purse, but she didn't pay for it."

Back in the classroom at last, Ms. Tracy tried to calm the children. But somehow, long vowel sounds couldn't compete with their class shopping trip. (And four more days of Book Fair Week!)

And so the day went: another "six hours of instruction" as she answered phone calls; wiped runny noses; found the thermometer to check for a fever; dug out the mother's phone number to come and pick up the sick child; phoned the office when she spotted nits on a little head; found some change to slip to Cassie so she could buy a sparkly pencil tomorrow; refereed arguments; redirected tattling; managed ADHD, OCD, and ODD; phoned to remind the office about the nits on the little head; and made it at last to the metal cabinet to find the birthday crown.

Their ordinary day climaxed at dismissal time when Mrs. Jones couldn't walk a straight line to pick up her child, Cassie. Ms. Tracy asked her politely, "Excuse me, Mrs. Jones, could you wait just a minute?" and elbowed the teacher dismissing beside her. "I need Mr. Pearson," Ms.

Tracy murmured under her breath. "Can you watch my students just a minute?"

The knot in Mrs. Tracy's stomach grew as the search for Mr. Pearson began. This was not the first time that this had happened with this mother. Next came Mr. Pearson's awkward conversation with Mrs. Jones . . . the phone call to another family member to come pick up Cassie . . . the explanation to Cassie, "Mommy's not feeling well today."

Ms. Tracy went back to her classroom to double-check the bathroom (just a thing she did), and make sure there was not a lost child cowering behind the waste can. As she was stacking the chairs for the janitor to sweep the room, an announcement came over the intercom: "Teachers, we will meet in the library in five minutes to analyze test scores."

Ms. Tracy scrambled to finish the chairs, feed the betta fish, and turn off the computer so she wouldn't have to come back to the room. She scribbled a note to remind herself to remind the office about nits on a little head, grabbed her purse and spelling tests, and headed for the library.

Just as she was going out the door, the phone rang. "Ms. Tracy, Kyle Sweeney's mother wants to know why he didn't get off the bus today."

"Kyle was absent today," Ms. Tracy replied, but not before she had nearly suffered a coronary. The "missed bus" phone calls ranked right at the top, even ahead of state audit interviews.

Late to the faculty meeting, Ms. Tracy slunk in the library door. Her pod partners were sitting at the corner table, guzzling caffeine. They had that glazed look in their eyes—that end-of-the-day look of a primary-grades teacher.

Just as Mr. Pearson was explaining that the numbers on the left meant that the students scored eleven points below the goal, she remembered the thought she'd been trying to complete.

The ratios—something is wrong with the ratios. "It is insane to put twenty six-year-olds in a classroom with one adult for seven hours a day and call it civilization," she whispered to one of her pod partners.

But her pod partner didn't hear her. She was bending over her sick card.

"Allergics," she wrote.

THROUGH HIS EYES

Mr. Pearson watched his faithful staff file into the library one at a time. His mind flashed back to his first year as a teacher and how honored and excited he had felt to be getting to work in his chosen profession, and with kids. His dream come true. His parents had been so proud of him. Yet he also remembered how rough that first year had been, as the reality set in, and the relentless daily grind took its toll.

And he remembered that day five years later when he cried on his way home from work as he realized he could not maintain what it took to be a classroom teacher much longer. That's when he went back to school to get his principal's certification. That's when he started feeling some new energy in his life again.

Mr. Pearson looked out over his team. There was Mrs. Hobson, now in her thirtieth year, and still one of the best fifth grade teachers in the region. Her husband Ed had died suddenly with a heart attack last summer. She often stayed after school to work in her room until the janitors locked up the building.

And over by the door was Mrs. Winger, talking a mile a minute to the others at her table. Mrs. Winger was in her third year and had become such an important part of this faculty. She was fighting cancer and would be starting treatments as soon as summer break started.

Sitting in the front, reading the paper while waiting for the meeting to begin, was Charlie, a first year kid who was a very gifted PE teacher. The students absolutely adored him. But he wouldn't be here very long, most likely. The school district had him coaching three sports, and Charlie had confided that he was applying for a teaching position in the next county over. The long hours were already wearing him down.

And just walking in was Billie, the school counselor. What Billie took home with her every night as she intervened day after day in the real lives of children from broken and dysfunctional homes would shock anyone who assumed she had a cake job.

As Mr. Pearson's eyes scanned the room, every one of his teachers suddenly seemed as if they were his sisters and brothers. Karen was illustrating the antics of one of her more rowdy students and had her table roaring. She had started out as a pretty weak math teacher, but had worked so hard to get more training, and had an excellent mentor in the person sitting next to her—Mrs. Johnson. At this stage Karen was invaluable to this team.

Mr. Pearson started to speak, but the words wouldn't come out. His voice quivered, and he cleared his throat. Finally, he simply said, "You guys are so special. What would this community ever do without this awesome group of teachers taking care of and loving on its kids? I don't have anything on the agenda today that I can't send out to you in an e-mail tomorrow morning. Go home. And from now on, let's do less after-school teacher's meetings. Oh, by the way, lunch this Friday is on me. I'm going to have the PTA help us, and we're having an afternoon celebration with the kids about just what you all mean to all of us. And one more thing. It is such an honor to get to be called your principal. You are such an inspiration to me. You are who get me going every morning. You are my heroes."

REFLECTIONS

1. How often does your school's staff stop to celebrate the great work that is going on all over your building every day?
2. What strategies could be put in place that would take the seemingly endless daily pressure off of your staff?
3. Has your school implemented regular culture checks and self-auditing of the daily non-instructional issues?

SOLUTIONS

In *Rocking the Boat* (Meyerson 2008), addressing the need for healthy change in the organization is gracefully presented with a "win win" approach. This attitude of "let's not be adversarial; let's just get better at what we do" is key. Far too often, those in the trenches who are living with toxic issues fear retribution if they come forward.

But, make no mistake: the dysfunction must be eliminated, or cultural cancer will continue. One of the key hurdles in any school that is truly embracing transformation and creating a culture that is both in the best interest of its students and also in the best interest of its faculty and staff, is to lay the reality on the table. When one school year finishes, what conversations need to take place that will prevent some of the same issues from cropping up the following year?

What can be done to improve classroom culture for both kids and teachers? Are adequate resources being allocated in age appropriate ways? Is the master schedule too complicated? Are classroom interruptions excessive? Can a volunteer program be developed which will provide able bodies for the early childhood program (and other age groups as well)? What innovative thinking can be tapped into to unchain the school to try bold, creative scheduling, and assignment of staff and students (and other resources)?

And, the discussion of the seemingly "engraved in stone" issues that are preventing what's best for kids from truly being practiced every day should not stop on the local school level. The discussion needs to be taken to the school district's board office, and then to board meetings, and on to regional and state meetings, and eventually to the state legislature . . . however many years it takes to get the attention needed to bring about change.

One person sounding the alarm can make all the difference. Several who have the solid research and evidence in hand will garner results even faster.

In many of the fifty states, it is not uncommon for one person to be considered adequate to care for five infants. (That's right: five babies. How many mothers of twins do not need a helping hand when their twins are infants? But *five*?) Up the scale the ratios go, with one adult being considered adequate to manage eight to ten two-year-olds or twenty six-year-olds. Even if those ratios were somehow safe for the children, what about the quality? Small children are needy, and their caregivers are often stretched beyond the breaking point. If our test scores are to show the results we are hoping for as a nation, we are going to have to aspire for more than crowd control in our early childhood classrooms. It is not only unrealistic, but it is also counterproductive to set the stakes high while keeping the support low.

NINE

Stella Rae

NAEYC STANDARD 4: USING DEVELOPMENTALLY EFFECTIVE
APPROACHES TO CONNECT WITH CHILDREN AND FAMILIES

*4c: Using a Broad Repertoire of Developmentally Appropriate Teaching/
Learning Approaches with a High Level of Cultural Competence, Understanding
and Responding to Diversity in Culture, Language, and Ethnicity*

Mrs. Carter loved her from the day she shuffled into her classroom — a respectful, quiet girl with learning challenges, and taller and heavier than any of her classmates. Mrs. Carter had never met a better listener. Stella Rae's big sister was raising her and all of her other siblings. They called her "Mom."

Mrs. Carter was advised by her colleagues from the beginning to have Stella Rae tested. That planted the thought in her head, and as Stella's learning difficulties became increasingly apparent, she grew more and more tempted. It was common knowledge in the community that this precious lamb was the product of generational incest. Though Stella Rae's father/grandfather's reign of terror on his family had finally ended at the graveside, he had left them with a long list of genetic challenges and a heavy load of emotional baggage.

It was early. Stella Rae had not yet been retained, but August is a hard month for teachers, and there was so much to do with the children who *were* ready.

Around September, Mrs. Carter referred Stella Rae to be tested for special education. She told herself she had done the right thing. Maybe her conscience wouldn't have bothered her if it all hadn't been done a little too fast. And by the time Stella Rae qualified for special ed, she had become a part of her classroom. Mrs. Carter's mouth fell open when the special education teacher came to tell her Stella Rae had qualified for special needs on the test.

When the day to sign the papers arrived, Mrs. Carter realized a step had been skipped—she had neglected to fill out that everlasting document where you list and date your interventions. Her guilt load got a little bit heavier. She tried to talk Stella Rae's big sister out of signing for a few more weeks, but special ed had been a positive and successful experience for her.

Sis signed the papers.

They came and got Stella Rae the next morning to go to the collaboration classroom for the day. Mrs. Carter watched her pick up her pencil and leave. She swallowed hard and thought, "It's the best thing for her." But her heart wouldn't catch up with her head. It kept lingering at the spot on the rug where her Stella Rae always sat at circle time. Though she struggled heart-wrenchingly at the reading table to put sounds together, it was Stella Rae who would raise her hand and answer the difficult questions at circle time on animal science and social studies comprehension.

Never, in all her years of teaching, had Mrs. Carter missed a child so badly. She missed her chunky, long form sitting so obediently; her serious, freckled face; her thoughtful answers; and her determined mind soaking up whatever she could like a little sponge.

Mrs. Carter went to the special ed teacher, Miss Maye, for reassurance. She knew Miss Maye was an excellent teacher, and the other children seemed to be thriving under her guidance, but perhaps their teachers had been more sure—perhaps their teachers had not hurried things. Mrs. Carter went to the Reading Recovery teacher to process. She, too, listened sympathetically. But the door had been shut; her Stella Rae was locked into her label. She prayed that God would help her get past this. Stella Rae was getting the attention she needed. Probably, they had done a good thing.

Then one morning while Mrs. Carter was greeting the children, Stella Rae's big sister asked if she had a minute. "Stella Rae wants back in your class. She's hasn't been wanting to come to school." Under normal circumstances, Mrs. Carter would have tried to talk her out of it . . . if it hadn't been for those interventions. (This time, she would do more; too many adults had already let Stella down in her young life. Mrs. Carter didn't want to be one of that number.)

"You know I may have to retain her," she said.

"It's okay, as long as she gets on your roster next year."

"I promise!"

A date was set for the ARC meeting, and Stella Rae's big sister signed her out of special ed. Mrs. Carter had her listener back. They worked very hard.

But the words still wouldn't come. On a defining day, Mrs. Carter put Stella Rae's reading book away and got out some old, classic starter books. Day after day, Stella Rae plugged away at those repetitive sight words. Night after night, Stella Rae's family reinforced her reading assignments. Stella Rae's confidence began to grow.

By the end of the year, Stella Rae could read over twenty beginner story books. "We're all so proud of her," smiled her big sister. In the old days, this would have been enough.

The next fall, Mrs. Carter's Stella Rae returned, towering over her new classmates. She started strong, as repeating children often do. But before long, Mrs. Carter saw that the reading was still challenging. Self-accusations flitted through her thoughts: *You should have been stronger about your decision. All you've done is lose a year for her. She's going to end up in special ed after all, and a year behind her peers.*

So she dug in with both heels and they hung on. Mrs. Carter made word matching games for her listener. She found interactive phonics games on the computer for her. She signed her up with the Title I teacher, and then the AmeriCorps worker. She did reading with her in her small group, and she did reading with her alone. And though she begged the Reading Recovery teacher, there was no loophole for a retained child to be serviced by the program. . . .

Mrs. Carter often wonders, with a hope that never ends, "Will Stella Rae ever make it in the regular classroom?" Perhaps someday she will work her way back in. There never was a harder worker. But for now, Mrs. Carter waves at her girl as she leaves for the morning with her small group.

Stella Rae smiles that shy smile, and the freckles pop out on her face. There's no way she can know the turmoil in Mrs. Carter's mind, the second guessing, the colleagues she has upset advocating for her girl, and the decisions she still questions.

But her smile seems to say, "I know you love me, Mrs. Carter. I know how hard you've tried." (You see, there never was a better listener.)

THROUGH HIS EYES

"If they all were only this dedicated," he thought to himself, as Mr. Pearson listened to Mrs. Carter pour out her soul over this one little girl. "But Stella Rae will be okay, Mrs. Carter. You have done all you can do. You've gone beyond the call of duty."

"No, I haven't, sir! She's like so many others who come to us from broken homes or from poverty. Too often they haven't been worked with at home on reading, and they don't even have children's books in the home. So, how would they even have the opportunity to be halfway caught up with the other children at school? All I'm asking is to be given more time to work with this child, and three others who are in a similar plight. Yes, they do have special needs—mainly, the special need of being loved and nurtured the way your children and mine have been from the day we brought them home from the hospital."

"But the referral process, Mrs. Carter. . . . We've followed the letter of the law on this, and we must let the system run its course. It all will work out in the end."

"Really? For little Stella Rae, it will all work out in the end? This little gal, Mr. Pearson, needs every ounce of intervention we can provide—from the time she hits the front door in the morning, until we put her back on the bus that evening. I was not able to provide near enough intervention. School had just started, my aide was out a lot with her own health issues, and quite frankly, I just didn't have a way to break down the instruction for all my kids in a way that met their very personalized and unique needs."

"But you did your best, Mrs. Carter . . . and I'm proud of you. That's all any of us can do."

"Well, I might have done my best with the formula for failure I was given to work with—too many at-risk kids in one room, too little time, too little help from instructional assistants, too many intercom and phone interruptions in my classroom off and on all day, too few art and music and recess and PE classes for my little ones if we are truly saying we are giving them our best."

Mrs. Carter began to cry. "Stella Rae, and so many others like her, need oh so much more than what our current structure provides, Mr. Pearson. Surely we can do better. I'm not your only teacher who goes home many nights frustrated with the reality that we are being asked to teach these kids to swim across a deep and wide river, when in reality they are barely ready to wade into a very shallow stream."

"I can't disagree with you, and what saddens me the most is after we work with these kids for six or seven years, as hard as we can with the resources we're allotted, we then send them on to another school and they soon fall further behind. So, it's like painting a house in the spring, and then by the time summer rolls around it looks faded and old again because we didn't use enough paint the first time. In the real estate business, they call it lack of TLC, or 'tender loving care.' In education, we call it 'the system,' or we blame it on the family. Either way, the end results are often very disappointing."

"I know, Mr. Pearson. I know. I've seen too many success stories—kids who rose above their less than advantageous circumstances to ever give up on a child . . . And I feel like I did somehow, certainly not on purpose, give up on Stella Rae way too soon."

"Don't you fret another moment about that, Mrs. Carter. I've been doing some thinking, and talking to other staff who feel as you do, and even looking into our budget. We do indeed have to provide more interventions in this school, from the get go . . . as soon as a student enrolls here, and in all classrooms; all grade levels. We're just not getting it done. And across the board, our entire school district is not getting it done. Our dropout rates from ninth through twelfth grade are embarrassingly high."

Mrs. Carter's mouth dropped open with pleasant surprise as Mr. Pearson went on. "So, I have checked with our central office, and there's a pot of money left over that I was supposed to receive at the end of the summer. We're going to pump all of it into our early childhood reading program. I think I can afford two additional aides, too."

"This is the best news I've heard in a long time, Mr. Pearson!"

"I apologize to you, Mrs. Carter. Oh how we've saddled you classroom teachers with an idiotic model, and expected you to somehow make it work."

"Thank you, Mr. Pearson. I know you're a caring principal, who works hard for this school and our kids, and for us, and the community. You're making a difference."

As Mrs. Carter left the office, Mr. Pearson turned in his chair and looked out the window. All these years, he'd mostly just buried his head in the sand when his teachers, parents, or someone else complained about how broken the system was. No more. He picked up the phone, called the superintendent, and simply said, "There's going to be some grant money coming along soon that will allow some schools to just throw away the mold and start over. As hard as we try here in this building, we're still losing ground. As soon as that grant is released, let me know, because, at this school, we're not playing the game anymore."

REFLECTIONS

1. What do you do in your classroom when you know a student needs much more "one-on-one" assistance?
2. What is your school doing to assist parents with providing a print-rich environment in the home?
3. How is your special education program set up to minimize the paperwork for teachers, and to maximize the interventions that are written into IEPs?

SOLUTIONS

In *The Differentiated School* (Tomlinson, Brimijoin, and Narvaez 2008), the classroom that goes far beyond "teaching to the middle" is detailed. The current climate across society, with an increased focus on the need for high-quality early childhood education, has the table set for schools to meet the urgent needs of our "babies" as never before. And, indeed, three- and four-year-olds are still babies. In a perfect world, we would have them stay home with their moms until age five or six, and then bring them to school for only a half day for the first year as they acclimated to being away from the security of a loving, educated home to the corporate structure of community school.

But this is not a perfect world. And, sadly, a high percentage of our little ones are not worked with at home in truly preparing them for "school." So, they come into this group setting, with its high-stakes testing and very structured daily routines, totally unprepared.

The most forward-thinking, child-centered schools of the future will develop strong foundational processes and incubators which will prepare kids thoroughly for their subsequent years of education (no matter what it takes). Students somehow being moved on to primary grades—even middle school and high school—who are still not able to read will be unheard of. Education models will be relentless about early childhood education. In fact, is there any other profession that somehow lets external pressures prevent the fundamental pieces from being ingrained first?

Can you imagine if the racehorse industry did this to its horses? "No, he's not ready to run in the Derby—no way. But, we've got to move on. Throw him in there anyway—he'll either 'sink or swim.'"

TEN

Boy Interrupted

*3a: Understanding the Goals, Benefits, and Uses of Assessment — Including Its
Use in Development of Appropriate Goals, Curriculum, and Teaching Strategies
for Young Children*

Maybe there was a reason why, as into aliens and pornography and
heavy metal as he was, Mayberry was his favorite place, and when no
one was watching, he slipped in an *Andy Griffith* episode now and then.

Maybe it was because something deep inside him knew it could have
been that way. These modern days had changed everything. In the old
days, dads stayed, Miss Crump set firm boundaries, and kids learned to
read with Dick and Jane. *Kids* learned to read; not babies.

Little kids stayed home and skipped rocks and kicked cans and
chased grasshoppers. Moms had time. You didn't even go to school 'til
you were six or seven (in his great-grandpa's day — eight or nine, even).
And nobody shot up with meth — there wasn't even such a thing.

Oh, these modern times. Drat these modern times — these great, en-
lightened, modern times.

Now and then, he could remember — something would trigger it — a
smell, a song, a rainy day sleeping in bed, some little thing would bring
back this foggy memory — him wrapped up in a patchwork quilt with his
dad. Big, muscular arms with black hair on them. The manly smell of his
dad's aftershave. Mom looking pretty and drinking coffee — Mom smiled

71

back then. He hadn't seen his mom smile in years. Them tickling him—both of them. Dad's big arms wrestling him.

He didn't know the big words then for what came next. Now he knew all too well: The furlough. The bankruptcy. And the meth. Mom scream-ing at Dad a lot. Dad's strong arms not tickling him anymore. Scared at night hiding under the patchwork quilt.

Andy would have worked it out, even with a furlough. Barney and Goober and Gomer and them would have rallied around him. They would have figured something out. Aunt Bea would have baked an apple pie.

And the school—that was the straw that broke the camel's back. It didn't have to be so hard. The doctor had told his mom he had at least an average IQ—*at least*. It didn't have to be so hard. Expecting him to read at five—it was the craziest thing. His first week of kindergarten, they sent home not only the traditional list of alphabet letters, but a long, long list of words to read as well (if he wanted to pass kindergarten).

The only word he saw was "tadpoles" at the science center. That was one word he cared about—bullfrog tadpoles, they were. He liked the way they hid under the rocks and grew legs and absorbed their tail (digested it, literally—that's why they weren't hungry for a while). He knew that when they kind of hung around near the top of the water, they were practicing their lungs, which would one day replace the work of their gills.

Bullfrogs could eat something as big as a small mammal. He could tell you that at five and explain to you what a mammal was, and that bull-frogs were amphibians, not reptiles like dinosaurs. Dinosaurs and rep-tiles were dryer and stuff than amphibians.

His teacher suggested that he had a learning disability and other is-sues, so he endured a battery of tests. The psychologist. The doctor visits. Andy Griffith and the gang would have chuckled and said to that teach-er, with all due respect, that it "wasn't nothin' a good dose of fresh air couldn't fix." They would have taken him fishing or something, and Pa would have given him a man-to-man talk, and they would have worked it out somehow.

It was humiliating—the round-robin reading. He figured out pretty soon that the teacher was going to give him the easiest page to read, so when it got close to the easiest page, he would go off to the bathroom. The bathroom became his best friend. He spent a lot of time in there, so he learned to fill it up with interesting pastimes like unrolling the toilet paper and stuffing it in the urinal, and urinating on the floor, and doing worse things on the wall.

It didn't have to be so hard. The doctor said his IQ was average—at least.

He had a lot of anger—the doctor said that, too.

He played video games and watched television all day. His mom tried to get him into sports. He hated it—all of those people watching him chasing that stupid ball around the field. After the first game, whenever she tried to make him go, he screamed, and kicked, and threw himself down on the floor.

Andy would have told him to get a grip, and chin up. Then he would have taken him out and passed a little baseball. Nobody had to make Opie play anything. He ran and played with the kids outside all day, and hiked in the woods, and grew things in his yard, and fished with his pa. And had chores to do—imagine that. Nobody had to sign him up at the "Y." The world was his gymnasium, and it was healthy and safe out there back then.

By fifth grade, Aden had decided that he was a loser, a little less capable than the others, a little less lovable, too—a boy without a dad, a disappointment to his mom, and a mistake. The only one he was right about was that he was a boy without a dad.

Sometime in eighth grade, he knew he wasn't going to stick it out to graduation. He found a gang of kids who felt the same way. They could be losers together. They found some ways to escape, none of which were safe, and most of which were illegal.

Aden's story isn't over yet. There are "Adens'" in every school, every grade, and every classroom. Whether we want to be or not, we are the actors as their story unfolds. Maybe we could choose to be a breath of fresh air like Thelma Lou, or a support person like the Pyle cousins, and by all means, in the name of common sense, an Andy Griffith. Or maybe we will just keep being aliens in a sanitized world, writing a meaningless script in a foreign language to a little boy who just needs to run outside and kick an old tin can around for a while. In the name of common sense.

THROUGH HIS EYES

The ARC meeting (the accepted common title for an Admissions and Release Committee meeting) dragged on and on, and Mr. Pearson shifted in his chair as he looked out the window. It had been a particularly long day, and as he desperately hoped that this official chatter which Aden's mother only barely understood would wrap up soon so he could go home to his family, an epiphany hit him like a cold glass of water to the face.

"Folks, please stop. As the chair of this committee, I have sat here for the last forty-five minutes and patiently listened to the buzz words, the education lingo, to this 'run-around' we are giving Aden's parent here again this year."

The eyes around the table all shifted to Mr. Pearson—wide-eyed and some mouths open. He went on. "Enough. We all know that we have not been fulfilling the details of Aden's IEP in the way it was worded and signed off on last year at this time. So, it's my turn to speak. Let's start over. Here's what I suggest we do. Let's take a look at Aden's world through his eyes—what a novel thought."

Mr. Pearson was noticeably irritated, his face was red, and his voice grew louder as he kept going.

"You see, I was a 'boy interrupted' as well, not unlike Aden in many ways. When I was nine years old, my dad lost his job as a bank executive and had to work two custodial shifts just to make ends meet. When I was twelve, we moved to a new town, a new school, and a new church. When I turned thirteen, my granddad suddenly passed away. When I was a sophomore in high school, I witnessed lifelong friends ruin their lives with alcohol and drug abuse.

"It was as if one day I woke up, and my carefree life as a young boy was gone. I found myself so depressed; so confused. For you see, I wasn't ready to grow up that fast. I wasn't ready to say goodbye to those magical days of childhood.

"How did I survive? I clung to my faith, my family, and my hobbies—and I lost myself in writing. My senior English teacher noticed that I had a gift, and all it took was her bragging on one of my stories the first week of school and I was off into another world. . . . A world that was safe and happy and . . . well, yes, my Mayberry.

"Quite frankly, that one teacher changed my life. I went on to college, and I learned to accept the uncertainties and pain of life, but to also celebrate the blessings.

"I can relate to Aden's world. He's not all that different, you know. In fact, we have perhaps a majority of our students here at this school who struggle with unique fears, loss of confidence, and learning styles which our faculty seemingly doesn't know how to address.

"So, here's what we're going to do. Write this down and put it in the plan, and I want us all to convene in exactly two weeks. In two weeks, if this IEP is not being followed, we'll do whatever we need to do to get Aden with the right people on my staff who still believe in Mayberry.

"For starters, I want Aden in a 'hands-on' science class, and I want him taken out of our experimental reading program. It is not working for him. I want him in Mrs. Shoemaker's room for at least one hour a day. I don't care how we do this, but she's the best reading teacher in the building, so why would we not have our at-risk readers working with her? I love the way she works with kids using the magazines and books that they enjoy the most. Aden will love Mrs. Shoemaker.

"Also, get Aden in our new intramural program. He'll love the focus on simply playing the game, and having less emphasis on trying to be a world class athlete at age ten.

"And, he needs field trips . . . field trips to museums, state parks, nature centers, caves, and hiking trails. Assign one of our new volunteer mentors to Aden and put it in this plan that we'll provide these trips— even if his homeroom isn't going. How hard could it be to take a van load of kids with unique needs, such as the ones Aden has, on some magical field trips?

"Finally, build into his plan that I will have breakfast or lunch with him here at school at least once a month.

"Now, tear that old IEP up—it's not worth the paper it's written on. I'm going home to my own 'Aden', who I just realized a few minutes ago is probably wondering why I've not taken him on a hike, or fishing, or golfing all fall. See you all in two weeks."

Rising from his chair, Mr. Pearson added, "Look at the time. Gee, we took an hour to play a game that doesn't work very well, and ten minutes to invent a process that will change a young boy's life—very doable strategies we should have known how to come up with when Aden was five years old."

Aden's mother sat with tears in her eyes, Mr. Pearson's staff sat dazed but proud of him. And as he drove home, he thought to himself, "It feels so good to be Andy. This is who I really want to be, and I'm not hiding it anymore."

REFLECTIONS

1. Are there "Adens" in your classroom or school who need to be given the blessing to just be kids again?
2. What processes in our educational sorting and intervention systems need to be made more practical and doable?
3. What areas in your school's total package of student services need more attention?

SOLUTIONS

Since the sweet days of *Sesame Street*, we have made progress in many areas. Class sizes are smaller (though still not small enough); inclusion for children with special needs is more and more a reality; earlier intervention increases the odds for at-risk children; we have Family Resource Centers to meet the needs of the whole child and family; teachers collaborate more than ever before . . . to name but a few of our improvements. But in some ways, we have gone backward.

In *Crisis in the Kindergarten* (2009), Miller and Almon address the pressure put on kindergarten teachers to produce high test scores in reading and math, although standardized tests are not even believed to be an appropriate practice with small children. Free-choice time at centers is becoming less and less a reality, as well as gross motor play time, while childhood obesity is now among the top three health problems of U.S. children.

Experts even worry about the social consequences we will pay for taking away children's play time—a necessary part of their mental, social, and emotional development. (As Piaget, Montessori, and Froebel each asserted, respectively, "Play is a child's work . . . play is the work of the child . . . play is children's work.")

By play, they were not suggesting a random, chaotic classroom. An effective early childhood teacher skillfully prepares his or her classroom environment with centers of carefully planned learning experiences that the exploring children will encounter. The most advanced children will be challenged. The delayed children will be stimulated. But no one will be frustrated.

This is no easy feat to pull off. But the fact is that when a child is pushed to read before his inner clock is ready, he may desperately try to tread water to keep from drowning. And in some cases, the "survivor," so to speak, never learns to read properly. This is not best practice.

In *Best Practice: Today's Standards for Teaching and Learning in America's Schools* (Zemelman, Daniels, and Hyde 2005), the authors outline an array of rich teaching/learning strategies that will motivate the schooling experience for any child, any age. We increasingly hear the phrase, "schools without walls," yet many schools still struggle with day-to-day processes which build even more barriers for students (and their teachers). A faculty could find amazing results if it would simply take a new, fresh approach in how it effectively delivers intervention strategies for every child.

From building more practical "real-life" strategies into IEPs, to recruiting volunteer senior citizen mentors, to planning virtual and "real-time" field trips for at-risk kids who have not had the cultural "basics" that we assume are commonplace throughout our culture, adopting a "school that cares" philosophy is a huge piece in the role we must play if we are to save more of our students from the abyss that shadows their lives.

But what about time? What about lack of resources? In this "school without walls," perhaps the school counselor is truly freed up from being an unofficial assistant principal or coordinator of assessment and is allowed to jump into the "real work" of intervening in the lives of at-risk students. Perhaps the PTA president is turned loose to refocus the energy of volunteers from fund-raising and dances to recruiting and training "mamaw and papaw buddies" who will come to school a couple of days a week to spend some one-on-one time with students who need role models and shepherds in their lives.

What if a school went back to the very beginning? What are the most important basic needs of the children and youth who come to that school? Immediately, the master schedule would reflect increased time for exercise and play, more art and music experiences (even if provided by volunteer coordinators), more special interest clubs, and more time for "life skills" training and support.

No longer would a high school senior reveal later that he or she had not met with a counselor several times to discuss various college and other post-secondary options. This very basic strategy would be built into every student's "life plan" as an essential, no longer limited to being a bonus experience for the savviest kids who have the most influential parents.

There are indeed innovative grants which allow for schools to go off the bureaucratic, mandated path to truly reinvent how they function. Those schools that leap into these waters will find amazing answers for the rest of us on how to truly be child-centered and life-changing for the students who are entrusted to our care.

ELEVEN
Lament of a Working Mother

NAEYC STANDARD 6: GROWING AS A PROFESSIONAL

6a: Demonstrating Professional Identification with and Leadership Skills in the Early Childhood Field to Think Strategically, Build Consensus, Create Change, Effectively Collaborate with and Mentor Others, and Have a Positive Influence on Outcomes for Children, Families, and the Profession

Dear God, I can't stop crying. Monday is coming, and I must go back to work. My new baby sleeps peacefully, unaware of the adjustment that awaits her. Oh, Lord, I think my heart will break. We've spent so many hours together, day after day, week after week, and she is completely dependent on me. I wanted for it to be different. I didn't want to love somebody this way.

When Megan was born, my whole family was in the waiting room, cheering us on. She was everybody's baby, and I've never felt less alone. I was on a cloud, floating high, and it was all like a dream; like a party. When her daddy and I took her home from the hospital, it was 50/50. *He* showed *me* how the nurses changed her diapers. But then reality hit, and everybody had to go home. Her daddy went back to work.

I didn't want to love somebody this way—but it happened. We were always together—she and I—hour after hour, day after day, week after week.

Oh, Father, what will I do? Monday morning, when she wakes up (she's a late sleeper), I won't be here, and it breaks my heart to think of how confused she'll be. She'll take a bottle—and it's my milk, anyway—

79

but never, ever has she had to go nine hours without nursing. She nurses for comfort. She nurses for security. It's about the only way she'll go to sleep.

How long is she going to cry for the comfort nobody can give her but me? She's too young to understand that I long to be with her—I'm just as gone as I would be if I wanted to be. And if I run into one more pampered princess looking down on me from her high horse, I think I'll scream. How dare they judge me as if I didn't love my child? *Please* . . .

People say stupid things to me like, "Are you excited about getting back to your classroom? I bet you've missed your students."

Right. While these postpartum hormones are raging through my system, while the milk is leaking from my engorged breasts, while I gaze upon the face of this sleeping cherub—our miracle, our gift from Heaven—all I can think about is my students. Right. (Please just send me one intelligent, honest woman, Lord. One who will rage with me about the injustice and stupidity of it all. Just one.)

I never thought about being promoted to this position of the most important individual in her life, her constant caregiver, her most treasured person. But she let me know in no uncertain terms that I was everything to her. Now I must step down and share my thorny crown with someone else—thorny because of the sleepless hours and constant self-sacrifice—a crown because it's just about the greatest thing I've ever experienced.

Oh, Father, the day she was born, she was everybody's baby. But as the days passed by, she chose me, and I fell in love. Help me, please help me. My heart is breaking.

THROUGH HIS EYES

Mr. Pearson had stumbled onto a very private reflection in a diary which one of his young teachers had left open on her desk. She had left early that day in a rush when the babysitter had called and told her that her baby was sick.

The next morning, during her planning time, he went down to her room. "Mrs. Livingood, have you ever considered easing into coming back to work by timesharing with another teacher?"

"What do you mean, Mr. Pearson? I don't quite follow you."

"Well, I've wondered about this on numerous occasions over the years, as my staff who are also mothers come back to work after having a child, and it seems as if they are torn between two worlds. What if I could help you build a bridge between those two worlds?"

"I'm all ears, Mr. Pearson. Go on." The young woman pulled her chair closer, and Mr. Pearson could see tears in her eyes.

"I have a veteran teacher who is hoping to retire, but she doesn't want to step away from teaching altogether. She would love to have the opportunity to work half days. If she could come in the mornings and work with your kids, and then you come in the afternoons, would you be receptive to such an arrangement? With your teacher's aide assisting her, I don't think it would be something she couldn't handle. In fact, she'd love it."

"Would I? Oh, Mr. Pearson, it would be a dream come true! I could be at home with my little one in the morning, then come here around lunchtime, then be back home with my family after school is out. . . . But what about your schedule here? Doesn't that leave you short a teacher?"

"Oh, we'll work it out. We need to be in the business of using common sense and finding solutions for you anointed souls who feel called to teach. Most always that means you're gifted and dedicated mothers as well. It's ludicrous for us to work you all as if you're in a factory producing a product on an assembly line. Give me a few days—I'm pretty sure our superintendent will let us try this out as a new model which might be offered across the school district later on."

Mrs. Livingood put her face in her hands and sobbed.

"I didn't mean to make you cry."

"Oh, no, sir! You've made me the happiest mother in the world!"

"Well, good, it's settled then. You go home and work out a plan with your babysitter. Will she be able to adjust to fewer hours?"

"Oh, I think so, since she's my mother."

As they both laughed, and Mr. Pearson headed toward the door, his young teacher stopped him. "Thank you. I was going to turn in my letter of resignation after this spring. My family comes first."

"I knew that might be what you were thinking."

Mr. Pearson went back to his office and called his wife. "Honey, I'm leaving work early today. Why don't you and the kids meet me at the pizza parlor for supper?"

"Okay, it's a deal. . . . Something happen at work today?"

"Yeah, I was reminded about what comes first. . . . See you in a few."

REFLECTIONS

1. Do you have staff in your school who would benefit from a time-share arrangement?
2. Does your school have a daycare for the children of employees?
3. What solutions do you offer for the dilemma our society struggles with in regard to having so many young mothers who work outside the home when their children are babies?

SOLUTIONS

In *The Power of Less* (Babauta 2009), the dilemma of overscheduling our lives is explored, with powerful alternatives offered. Every teacher would benefit from embracing this concept of "the power of less." And for teacher/mothers, the paradox of teaching the masses while also taking care of a family is an ethical dilemma indeed.

Yet teachers who are also mothers often don't hold the trump card in fixing the dilemma of being sent right back into the classroom just weeks after their own babies are delivered. And many, many resent the "system" for using them, as if they should understand the paradox of taking care of everyone else's children, but not having time to raise their own.

The rigidness of retirement systems and the industrial age mentality of school calendars and master schedules add to the problem. But, working mothers can help us come up with better answers. In a time when all eyes are focused on how schooling models need to be overhauled, innovative solutions for how to best utilize the skills of our young teachers who are also mothers are just waiting to be explored.

As we face the reality of how far behind many of our preschool kids are, due to not having the steady support of their own parents at home, may we practice what we preach, so to speak, and create family-friendly cultures for our teacher parents to work in. We have huge pools of trained teachers out of work due to current economic conditions who would treasure a part-time assignment. We have "stay at home" moms who would enjoy assisting as an aide for a few hours a week.

Perhaps we've over-regulated the "system." Perhaps we need to re-think how we stress "career," but seem to have lost touch with the price-less relationship between mother and child.

In exploring avenues that would allow for much more flexibility for teachers who are also mothers of young children, shouldn't we begin by talking to the mothers themselves? They will have an abundance of good, doable suggestions. In this age of overhaul of many of our bureaucratic "systems" across our culture, this is another example of the old para-digms needing renewal.

TWELVE

They Have Parents

NAEYC STANDARD 2: BUILDING FAMILY AND COMMUNITY
RELATIONSHIPS

*2b: Supporting and Engaging Families and Communities through Respectful,
Reciprocal Relationships*

Though a first-year teacher, Miss Rodriguez astounded her colleagues
with her abilities, passion, and impressive test scores. Her biggest challenge from day one, however, was to understand the parents' view. She
thought of them as pests and dreaded their phone calls and visits until
the last day of school her first year, when one of the mothers gave her a
story about her small son, written from her heart, and illustrated with
photos. Miss Rodriguez lay in her bed that night and read the tribute
over and over.

IN CELEBRATION OF GABRIEL

And God said, "Let there be dimples. Place twinkling, blue eyes and an
infectious, little grin on an irresistible face. Pour blond curls all over his
head. Don't forget to leave a space between his front teeth so his smile is
as unconforming as the rest of him. Put dimples on the elbows, too. Make
one that thinks outside the box. He will leap. He will skip. He will bound.
He will hop. He will ask more questions than could ever be answered,
and in a husky, little voice.

Wind him up. Charge his batteries; batteries that never stop. Show him the colors of the rainbow. My eagles flying on the wind. The tadpoles in the puddles. More wonders to explore than there are hours in the day. And whisper in his ear, 'Jesus loves you.'" And the evening and the morning were the ninth month. And God saw that it was good.

When I talked my husband into a third baby, we didn't even think about the gender. When people said, "What do you want it to be?" I thought, "I want it to be a baby; a precious, cuddly, sweet-smelling, little baby!"

On the way to the ultrasound, I ventured to ask Gene, "Do you have a preference?"

"I like my little girls," he said. If he had ever had that age-old, male need to re-create himself, it had vanished at the first sight of his newborn girl—dark skin, cleft chin, spiked hairdo—the prettiest baby that had ever been born (as every parent's baby is). Her gentle spirit wrapped itself around our hearts with an eternal grip. He was smitten.

Then came his second daughter (the other prettiest baby ever), all chubs and curls. She was a thousand laughs a day, mischievous, curious, a fat, beautiful, little giggle-box. Her daddy (and I) fell headlong in love again.

When they told us the third one was going to be a boy, I laughed. Gene was pretty much speechless all of the way home.

Gabriel started out just like his sisters, a sweet, little, angel-like bundle. He and Whitney (then six) fell asleep in the rocking chair together the day we brought him home from the hospital. (That was the last quiet day I remember.)

Four years later, there are little experiments set up all over our house. "Why are you bringing all of that water outside in the cold, Son?" "Because I want to see it turn to ice." (It did.) My kitchen is now a small chef's workroom. He mixes pudding, coffee grounds, flour, cereal, and minced onion. "Mommy, this is for you to eat."

"Yum!"

Every day, we must boil an egg (or twelve), but not for the chef—for the artist. Always, always, there are cups of colored water on my work table and boiled eggs soaking in every glorious combination of colors.

We have our most scientific and theological talks as we are driving to work. Gabriel wants to know how people make guardrails, road signs, and traffic lights. "How do people make the road?" he would ask me almost every day when he was three.

I have to think about things I've never thought or cared to think about before. I think I did okay on the one about the road. But *traffic lights?* "They use electronics," I venture. "They use electricity and lightbulbs, and plastic or glass or fiberglass." (Well, what do *you* think they use?)

Gabriel wants to know how *God* makes things. "How did God make the moon?" he asked on the way to school one morning. (Gabriel is the scientist. I am the theologian.)

That one was easy. "Well, God said 'Let there be light,'" I said with tears in my eyes. "And there was light. A sun [to rule by day] and a moon [to rule by night]."

"Neat!" came my small companion's enthusiastic voice from the back of the van. Then . . . "How did God make the moon?"

The other morning, on our one-minute walk from the parking lot to our daily destination, Gabriel pointed out three of the wonders of nature to me. "Look, Mommy, a flower! See the bird flying in the sky? I see the sunrise!"

"Yes, Gabriel, look!" I said, hugging him a little closer. (Why must everything commence at such a tender, morning hour?) Probably, it's good he couldn't read my thoughts, for I don't see sunrises on that one-minute walk. I see a dream that is slipping away. *Dear God, my Father, it was such a simple, little dream,* I whisper. *Was it so very much to ask?*

"Good morning, how are you?" smile the people.

"Fine, how are you?" I smile back. *Dear God, my Father, where do I put this rage and sorrow?* (I had plans for the baby years, and breadwinning wasn't one of them.)

"Tell me about God and the debil [*sic*] and power," Gabriel says (like he did yesterday . . . and the day before) on the way home from school. "The debil just has a little bit of power."

(Power? Where did he hear about power? It must be a boy thing, and it must be born in them.)

"That's right, Gabriel, and only because God gave it to him. Someday, when Jesus comes to take us home, God will take away even that little bit of power."

"And then the debil will be sad."

"Yes, Gabriel. And everything will be all right."

"Mommy, are you tired?"

"Yes, I'm very tired."

"I'm not tired. I'm *nebber* tired!" (Words more true were never spoken.)

He thinks outside the box. If someone asked me, "Who is your friend at school?" I would say, "Dianna . . . or Chris . . . or Jenni . . . or Shannon."

When we asked Gabriel that question his first week of preschool, he said, "Josephina." (Pronounced /hosufeena/.)

I trustingly commented to his teacher, "Gabriel told me about his little friend, Josephina." His teacher looked at me kindly. "We don't have a Josephina," she said. *(But we do, I remembered suddenly: one of the girls' dolls.)*

When he transferred to another classroom during the second week, I asked him, "Who is your friend?"

"Juanita," he promptly replied. (That's his grandmother.)

If I had a speech teacher to help me pronounce my words right, and my mother asked me, "What does your speech teacher look like?" and she was pretty and had dark hair, I would say, "She is pretty and has dark hair."

"What does your speech teacher look like?" I asked Gabriel.

"A dinosaur," he answered without slowing down from his play.

"What did you have for breakfast at school?"

"Pizza." (I know nothing, absolutely nothing about his school except for what I find out on my own. And that there is a froggie—a huge froggie—huger than his teacher, and his teacher won't let him bring it home.)

His favorite part of his favorite song is *Jesus Loves Me When I'm Bad*. But he can be so very good and kind if we need a hug or Jacqui Rebecca stubs her toe. He can clean his room. He can dress himself. And he asked Jesus into his heart when he was three. "I'm a Cwistian [*sic*]," he tells me.

"I know you're a Christian, Gabriel." (Thank goodness it's about grace.)

He has moments of insight. "Nebber [*sic*] say 'stupid,'" he admonished a little peer the other day. "'Hands are for helping, not hurting.'"

We planted our flowers on April 14. I know the frost will get them, but Gabriel couldn't wait another day, and besides, it will be fun to plant them all again. He has six flowers growing in his room: two mums, two primroses, and two impatiens. "May I please have one flower?" he asked politely as I was planting. "Thank you. May I please have one more? May

I please have one more?" Beside the outside-flowers-growing-inside is a bowl of tadpoles. His sandbox is sprouting pumpkins.

I promise.

Well, they're not *in* the box, exactly (and neither is anything else about Gabriel—nothing is *in* the box), but they are in the mud pile *outside* his box. He had this cup of waterlogged pumpkin seeds he had saved from his decorative pumpkin last fall. He saved them all winter. Sometime this spring, he "planted" them by pouring the whole cup of pumpkin seeds in one big pile in the mud by his sandbox. We patted some mud over some of the seeds.

This week, I saw the sprouts. I laughed. Today, they were quite large and leafy. I laughed some more. Gabriel's first garden—a pumpkin patch "out of" his sandbox.

He's going to plant an apple tree, too. Actually, he already has. There were seeds from his apple. I'm watching for the sprout.

The other day, I was doing some of my in-the-box things (and *smothering in there* , and a Dr. Seuss photo caught my eye: 1904–1991. That guy lived eighty-seven and a half years, and one of his friends called his death "untimely." *You know why he lived so long, Lord?* I whispered from inside the box. Sure, He knew. (Dr. Seuss didn't live in a box, you know. Neither does God.)

Gene and I are both about ten years older than we were four years ago. But sometimes I look at our son and say, "Can you believe what we would have missed if we hadn't had him?" (Gene is still speechless.)

Go ahead, third child. Run, bound, leap, fly. Perhaps, some day (sooner than later), our wings, too, will catch the wind.

And God will say, "It is good. It is very good."

> I will praise Thee, for I am fearfully and wonderfully made, marvelous
> are Thy works; and that my soul knoweth right well.
> —Psalm 139:14

When school started the following August, young Miss Rodriguez's attitude toward parents was noticeably softer. And when Mr. Pearson asked the teachers to write a resolution for the coming year, Miss Rodriguez simply wrote, "I resolve to try to see each student through a mother's eyes."

THROUGH HIS EYES

After his young teacher had shown him the parent's story about her son, Mr. Pearson simply smiled. "You're going to have a great year, Miss Rodriguez." And he thought to himself, "What an invaluable lesson this could be for candidates in teacher prep programs—long before they are actually given their own class."

Early the next morning, Mr. Pearson picked up the phone. A buddy from college, Charles Young, was supervising the field/clinical work of student teachers at a nearby university. As Mr. Pearson explained his request, he could hear the excitement on the other end of the line.

"So, Pearson, you would actually allow me to assign students in our teacher prep program to your school, much earlier than their student teaching year, but with the stipulation that they will spend half of their time interviewing and working with parents?"

"Yes Charles. That's all I'm asking. I have realized, through the experiences of one of my own new teachers, that unless they have children of their own, there is no way they can understand the full scope of what we're asking them to do. I want to immerse them in a much deeper understanding of motherhood, and the priceless gift every parent 'loans' this school every day."

"I love the concept. I'll talk to our dean, and call you back later this week. How will you recruit the parents who would be a part of this project?"

"That won't be hard to do. All of our early childhood teachers do home visits regularly, and have great relationships with the mothers of our young students. We'll get permission to video some of the conversations too, so you can share them in your other education courses."

"But there is a downside to this brainstorm of yours, Pearson. You do understand that with an increase in such 'up-close' exposure in the real school setting so early in the teacher prep program, we'll lose some candidates. They will realize that this might not be what they are cut out for as a career."

"Hmm, interesting. Is that so bad, to help them to not make a poor vocational choice so young in life?"

"No, it's not. Actually, the principals and superintendents in our region will love this. They have been scolding me for a while now that we are still sending them too many education majors who do not have the dispositions to be in the classroom. . . . Pearson, you're a piece of work."

"I'll take that as a compliment, Charles. Call me when you get the green light. I want to start this program this fall."

REFLECTIONS

1. Is the process for mentoring student teacher candidates and first year teachers who are assigned to your school thorough and effective?

2. Do you think new teachers have time to develop authentic relationships with the parents of the children they work with? How often does your school require home visits?

3. Are the teachers in your school strategically assigned to the various student age-groups based on their experience working with children? Or, are assignments routinely made based on seniority and a "rites of passage" mentality?

SOLUTIONS

In *The Advantage* (Lencioni 2012), organizational health is explained as the variable that takes precedence over everything else. When toxic culture and dysfunction are dealt with, needed change is cultivated. Too often the schooling process turns into a corporate world mentality, with a tendency toward industrial-age thinking and a factory-like approach. Central office directors, principals, and teacher leaders don't do this necessarily on purpose, but tight budgets, pressurized master schedules, and the need to label and sort too often result in school processes that work for the adults in the building much more than for the students and their parents.

Major transformation can take place, sometimes even without increased funding or staff, when professional educators take the time to have honest conversations about the blind spots in their own work. Talking to parents—really talking to parents—and getting to know them well is a great place to start. The medical field is now embracing the concept of patient input. The business field stresses customer service. The church understands its role is largely about the needs of the community. And

highly effective twenty-first-century schools will be rigorous about
breaking down walls—whatever it takes to get to the most important
issues of "children first."

THIRTEEN

Come August

NAEYC STANDARD 4: USING DEVELOPMENTALLY EFFECTIVE APPROACHES TO CONNECT WITH CHILDREN AND FAMILIES

4d: Reflecting on Own Practice to Promote Positive Outcomes for Each Child

> Though no one can go back and make a brand new start, anyone can start from now and make a brand new ending.
>
> —Unknown

Picking off the petals of a daisy, Loraine chanted the old refrain (but revised to meet her personal battle), "I am a good teacher, I'm not a good teacher. I am a good teacher; I'm not a good teacher."

This was not a midlife crisis for her. She had been through this same struggle almost yearly since the tender age of twenty-two. And many times a year, she wondered how she had wandered into the field of education and why she hadn't spent more time choosing a career. What she had wanted to be when she grew up was a missionary, a newspaper editor . . . or an Olympian.

But every August, the call of bare bulletin boards in need of back-to-school displays, the smell of fresh paint in the primary colors, and the memory of little hands reaching for her compelled her to come . . . back home.

Sometime around mid-year, she was spent. By May, she was always more than spent—she was a volcano of emotion ready to erupt; the epitome of burnout, stress, and depression.

In June, she always began the process of recovery: Healing sleep. Deep-cleaning. Peaceful hours in her flower garden. Making memories with her children. The days of the calendar flew by with a fury in those long-anticipated months of summer.

And then came August. . . . And the call of the classroom. . . . This year, it would be different. This year, she would stay focused.

So many distractions as the journey of her life played out its stages. First, the all-consuming experience of falling in love. The wedding. The miracle of bringing children into the world. Inexpressible joys and count-less needs. The maternal drive to be home with them. Buying and selling a home. Financial stress. Teenagers and graduation. The first one to leave the nest—oh, that knocked the breath out of her! And each time, with each nestling that spread its wings, she hurt in new ways.

College tuition. More college tuition. Aging parents. Their passings—worse than the empty nest. No one could have prepared her for this kind of grief—trying to get her footing again. Picking up the phone to check on Mom or Dad before she remembered . . . they're gone.

Perhaps the only thing in her life that stayed the same was the school calendar year and her roller coaster emotional cycle. Climbing up, up, up the tall mountain in August, the giddy ride downhill as she and the children connected in September when her favorite topics were still be-fore her, and the new saddle oxfords under their eager desks were still unmarred. And then the next climb, each mountain higher as the year marched on and the daily grind got weary.

Then it came—the bad mammogram. Happens all of the time . . . and to lots of teachers. Whether it's from the stress, the long-term sleep-depri-vation, or the delayed motherhood is a toss-up. For her, it was probably all three. (She had long dreamed of having a surgery in April. Just the right time to skip the whole spring fever ordeal—you know—the kids are climbing the walls and the teachers are pulling their own hair out. Just the right time for a good rest. She had always liked hospital food. Hey, she would never sneeze at anything brought in to her on a tray—talk about king-living!)

Cosmic humor would have it that she got sick in September—how very unfair. By then, everyone knew what bus to ride, while the crayons in their boxes still had the sharpened points.

She didn't pull any punches—the chemo, the mastectomy, the radia-tion, the reconstructive surgery.

The nausea was awful. And that heaviness in the night—that gripping fear that she wouldn't be there for the rest—her daughters' childbirths, the delights of grandchildren, growing old with her husband. But the nagging fear she had not expected was that she would never resolve the haunting dilemma: "I am a good teacher. I'm not a good teacher." (The daisies had never been consistent in their answer.)

Her answer came in a letter written to her by her oldest child, the one for whom she had felt that first searing pain of separation upon her return to work a few weeks after the birth. The one over whom she had sobbed so long through that first night before work that her eyelids were swollen the next morning.

Dear Mom,

I know you're going to beat this thing. But in case you need a little encouragement between battles, I just wanted to let you know some of the reasons I always wanted to be like you.

I have always thought you're beautiful. Not in a Liz Taylor sort of way, but in the way your eyes close softly when you hold a sobbing child. In the way your face got that determined look as you dug through our outgrown clothes for dresses that would fit that neglected, little girl in your classroom. The times I saw tears trickle down your cheeks over a child who had touched your heart, and the compassion on your face when you worked with your struggling readers. Oh, Mom, how hard you fought to keep them afloat!

I know your teaching career has had its highs and lows. And I know your worst fights with Dad have been over leaving us with a sitter. But I think the very thing you have struggled with all your life has shaped you into a beautiful person. You have grown into one of the most patient people I have ever known—and that didn't come easy for you.

You have fought vehemently for the rights of children. You have been an unpopular advocate at times, but oh, Mom, how I have always admired you with that fire in your eyes!

And perhaps the greatest lesson you have ever taught me is that of perseverance. I know you did it mostly for us, and mostly to put bread on the table. That is love. But in your life work, you kept falling in love with other children, too. Thank you for showing me that a mother's heart is not like a closet that can only hold so much love, and then the door must be shut. But it's more like a spreading vine that keeps giving and giving, climbing and reaching out beyond its cozy little garden to the wide, wide world out there.

I love you for being so human, Mom. For how long it took you to
overcome your temper and your . . . shall I say . . . "articulate tongue"?
How you became like the Proverbs 31 woman, "On her tongue is the
law of kindness." I love you for loving us so fiercely, for all the second-
guessing you did of yourself, for your humble heart, and for your big
heart.

I love you, Mom. For to those who know you well, your life is an
open book. And you are the best teacher I know.

Megan

She creased the tear-stained letter into her lesson-plan book, for the call of
the classroom was knocking on her door again. The back-to-school sales
were beckoning her. The fresh smell of school-bus yellow paint was in
the air. And she had a bulletin board just begging for a new splash of
color.

Apples, maybe, she would do this year, or a flower garden with the
children's names and sweet faces on the blooms. And the teacher—maybe she would be a vine this year—spreading, climbing . . . beyond her
little garden.

THROUGH HIS EYES

Mr. Pearson sat back in his chair and rubbed his eyes as his last teacher
interview had just wrapped up. He had decided at the end of the last
school year to take extra time this year to sit down with every one of his
staff and let them share whatever was on their mind.

After several weeks of squeezing these conversations in amidst the
always hectic school calendar, he now had his evidence. He was not
really surprised by what had been confirmed, but was somewhat disillu-
sioned that more of his staff had not come to him and confided about the
many issues they were dealing with. So, he grabbed his notepad and
hurriedly developed a staff support plan of a different kind. He had
wanted to do this for years, and scolded himself for taking so long.

Holistic Plan for Taking Care of My Team

- Schedule one-on-one "conversation" time with each staff member
  at least once each semester, and use this time to discuss their pro-

fessional development needs (from their perspective, and include their life stressors).

- Get out of the office more, and get to know my people and their "life stories" better.
- Schedule regular after school sessions which address very specific needs and insecurities that teachers will naturally have about their work. These should be more about support—not so much about the technical skills that they routinely get training on anyway.
- Utilize teacher's meeting time for book studies and discussions about those "real-life" issues in and out of school that can impact a teacher's work in stressful ways.
- Teacher "dispositions," effective relationships, and emotional intelligence—spend more time providing training in these "soft-skill" areas. I should never have a teacher or other staffer drowning on my watch, and not have provided unwavering support for the holistic needs of that person.

REFLECTIONS

1. Does your principal or school's support process provide time for discussion of your other teaching issues, other than student achievement and assessment strategies?
2. Professionally, do you have a mentor or critical friend who you regularly go to to discuss the ups and downs of your career?
3. What questions/doubts/fears do you struggle with about your work, and how could these be better addressed?

SOLUTIONS

In *Courage to Teach* (Palmer, 2007), the author bares the soul of a caring teacher—the good days and the bad, the euphoria and the array of frustrating emotions. And perhaps we've added to the internal contradictions of the teacher with our strange selling out to the corporate model. Schools are not factories. They are not a mall, airport, or stadium filled with faceless people. They are communities. But for whatever reason, we've allowed them to become impersonal, almost too cookie-cutter, and perhaps even almost too strategically designed to be intricately involved in the real worlds of the students and staff. How tragic.

The original "schoolhouse," the one room model like what is portrayed in the old *Little House on the Prairie* episodes, was all about community. Every student knew every other student and their family. The teacher was intricately involved in this community culture. "School" was life, just like the community store, the community church, the community post office.

Somehow, we've "evolved" (or is it "de-evolved"?) from the school as a small, close-knit community, to the school as the storehouse of knowledge. In reality, it is a "big brother"—very stoic, very impersonal at times—in fact *not* meeting human needs to such a degree that close to 30 percent of high school students drop out.

Students, teachers, other staff, and parents so need, and deserve, to be a part of the authenticity—the "realness"—of a true community school. Those visionary leaders who will forge this course, despite fierce opposition from some who incredulously think the "system" is in good shape, will help turn the tide for the rest of us, and it can't come too soon.

FOURTEEN

Educating the Masses

NAEYC STANDARD 6: GROWING AS A PROFESSIONAL

6e: Engaging in Informed Advocacy for Children and the Profession, Skillfully Articulating and Advocating for Sound Professional Practices and Public Policies

"So *that's* what all this is about!" thought Miss Mollett after reading about *Sputnik* in her night class. "Russia sent up the first Earth-orbiter way back when (the nerve of them!). And America has been scrambling ever since. This explains why we're trying to teach our babies to read before they know their alphabet."

And now, to add insult to injury, China . . . and India. Moving ahead. Or so they would lead us to think. "Aren't there starving children wandering the streets of India?" Miss Mollett whispered to herself. "And we're *jealous?*"

She thought back to the extravagant show of "wealth" and "power" China had put on at the recent Summer Olympics. What was the ungodly estimate of expense for their fireworks display and other fluff, 40 billion dollars? Miss Mollett had felt her blood boil when she thought about the many Chinese children who were locked away in sweat shops, slaves for this industrial "giant" of a nation as it flexed its financial muscles for all the world to see, and she was not impressed.

A child advocate to the bone, Miss Mollett was accustomed to feeling that lonely old companion, Cynicism, breathing down her neck at what should have been enjoyable celebrations. She was always uncomfortably aware that the toys that were passed around at her family's cozy Christmas celebrations had been made by child labor in developing countries. (The little people's toys and the big people's toys. There was a reason she bought her laptop used. And wore tarnished earrings. And stopped eating chocolate. A lonely little boycott was hers, but an informed conscience can be a hard master.)

Now, as her professor and classmates discussed *Sputnik*, Miss Mollett felt the wheels of her mind begin to turn even faster, and another connection snapped into place. "No wonder they always give us such a run for our money in the Olympics," she thought. "When you trim off the 'cream of the crop,' and educate that small portion and them alone, while you throw away the rest of the crop—the vast majority—the poor children, then what do your test scores prove? Rather small sampling, ey?"

"We educate our masses," Miss Mollett heard herself say, and noticed a couple of classmates glance her way. (They were talking about the economy now.) ". . . In a nation where every child is entitled to a free, public education." She closed her eyes and remembered her Nellie, a smile playing at the corners of her mouth while a tear trickled down her cheek.

"My Miss Mollett," Nellie would say every morning as she worked her way into the kindergarten classroom behind her walker. Things would get in the way. Table edges. Rugs. Other students' feet.

"Move over, Nellie. You have to go around it," Mrs. Chapman, her ever-faithful special-needs aide, would say.

"Yeah," Nellie would say as she made her way to the rug for the morning story time.

"Trains!" Nellie would call as the other children gathered on the rug. Nellie's favorite story was the old classic about the little blue engine who thought she could . . . and did.

It was always hard for Miss Mollett to correct Nellie, even when Nellie called out without raising her hand, or held onto Miss Mollett's arm and teased her while she was trying to put a star on their papers. When Miss Mollett felt that little hand wrap around hers and saw the dimples shining, she felt her heart melt. Always.

For Nellie was no ordinary child. When First Steps had made their first home visit, Nellie was basically lying on the floor all day staring into space. In preschool, she learned to sit up in a wheelchair. By kindergarten, she was on a walker. In first grade, the physical therapist said, "Nellie will walk."

How Miss Mollett had grown to love the sound of Nellie's walker coming down the hall. She never knew a more indomitable spirit in a child. It was work to get anywhere, but Nellie never gave up. The day Miss Mollett put her and her walker inside the kindergarten line, Nellie giggled all the way to the cafeteria.

The class slowed down for her.

"We've got time," Miss Mollett said.

After that, there was no turning back. Nellie was part of the line, no longer traveling by herself and Mrs. Chapman. She never ceased to get the giggles over the thrill of it all.

Miss Mollett's graduate school classmates were now discussing de constructing the standards, and Miss Mollett tried hard to tune in, but she kept hearing Nellie's laughter. It was the day the maintenance men installed her special swing on the playground. The whole kindergarten class gathered around and applauded as Mrs. Chapman lifted Nellie into the swing. The same way they had done when William, the tall, gangly boy from Gitchen Holler, learned to write his name, and when Jessica, who had been born addicted to drugs, learned to identify the letter "Aa." There was a lot of love in that classroom.

Nellie walked. She walked before the second grade. The office called Miss Mollett in her kindergarten classroom to tell her that Nellie had made it to the cafeteria without her walker.

It had been a gradual thing. First she walked through the pod with Mrs. Chapman by her side. Next she went down to the janitor's closet, and then a little farther. Today she made it.

Miss Mollett left her students with her kindergarten aide and went to the cafeteria. She wrapped her arms around Nellie and wept. Nellie patted her head and said, "My Miss Mollett."

That was the same year the state took over the school. Their test scores had not risen fast enough, and they had entered their fifth year of "decline." Half the faculty, including Miss Mollett, lost their jobs.

But Nellie had walked. William had learned to write his name. Jessica began her journey through the alphabet. And the masses were educated.

THROUGH HIS EYES

As Mr. Pearson watched Miss Mollett clean out her room and load up the back of her fiancé's truck, his stomach ached for her, and for all of his staff. There had been no other school year like this one. Normally, on the last day of school, the staff would gather in the cafeteria for an end-of-year party, and to honor any retirees.

Everyone would be laughing and feeling the stress leave their bodies as they celebrated another eventful, impacting school year, and the beginning of summer. It was time to rest; time to be at home with their kids; time to help with Vacation Bible School at church; time to help haul kids to camp; time to spend hours at the ballpark; time for swimming at the neighbor's pool; and time to help Mamaw and Papaw with their garden and canning.

But not this summer. No, this summer, the school was, in essence, being taken over by others who had determined that it was not fit to remain intact. Hadn't made the "passing grade." So, by statute, half the staff was let go, and new teachers fresh out of college were being brought in. Yes, they would be the answer! They would know how to teach! With outside help, this school would be turned around in no time—at least in a way that got the results needed to play the game.

Mr. Pearson swallowed hard, and called his wife. It was time. When he got off the phone, he felt like he'd just been let out of prison. Then, he called the superintendent. He'd wondered what it would feel like when this day came. He had butterflies . . . he wanted to take his kids fishing as soon as he got home . . . he wanted to take his wife to dinner and a movie. In fact, he was so excited he had to pinch himself when the super's voice came on the other end of the line so he could speak calmly and not with laughter and uncontrolled yelping—what he was feeling all over as his body trembled.

"Sir, I just wanted to thank you for being so, so good to me all these years. I have much respect for you. You're a good man. And so I know you'll congratulate me when I share this news with you. I'm retiring this summer. In fact, I'm retiring this week."

"Mr. Pearson, I'm shocked. But what about the school? What about all the plans that have been made to re-invent it? What about . . . ?"

"Sir, what school? We died today, remember?"

"But things will change, I promise. Just hang in there with us for another year or two. Let's pull off a miracle."

"Pull off a miracle, sir? We were pulling off miracles. This school has an 80 percent free and reduced lunch count, and 12 percent of our student population is special needs. Yet our attendance rate this year was again near 94 percent. Our discipline referrals went down for the third straight year. Our PTA membership was up. Our student clubs increased. Our volunteer hours increased. And our test scores held their own."

"But that was the problem. They just held their own—still under the bar that has been established, Mr. Pearson. You know that."

"Yep, I do indeed know that—the assessment was the problem, sir."

"But that's not what I mean."

"But it's what I mean. Here's the reality, sir. We are a rural school, with bus routes that pick some kids up at 6:30 a.m. and don't get them home 'til 5:00 p.m. Most of our families live in isolation and poverty. We have not been given an increase in teacher assistants for several years now, even though in our strategic planning we have asked for additional staff support over and over. One of my worst teachers, and one who is known to berate and belittle her students, was left here despite my efforts to at least have her transferred to another school and to work with older kids who maybe could handle her harassment a little better."

"But Mr. Pearson!"

"Please let me finish, sir. . . . Last year, my budget was cut for the fifth straight year, and thus we lost our art teacher. This year, we were cut yet again and I'm losing my PE teacher. We share our music teacher and band director—the same person—with two other schools. We have no one to help coordinate the new intramural program we've tried to get going, so our volunteer coaches gave up on it, and it's folding.

When we were passed over last summer on a huge reading grant, I lost one of the best teachers I've ever hired to the school in town. We have needed a new, modern playground for ten years, but when I asked the board for assistance, they suggested we do fundraisers. My PTA president resigned on that one."

"Perhaps you all have been given a stacked deck of cards. I don't disagree. But think of what can happen from this point on! Think about the potential for your students to succeed, and be somebody in life."

"With no disrespect, sir, they are already somebody in life. And they have been nurtured and cared for day after day, year after year, by a very dedicated faculty—however understaffed we have been, and however ignored our requests for the right kinds of help. Don't you get it, sir? The system is broken. No, I do not have perfect teachers. But I do have a vast majority of good teachers, talented teachers, teachers who love these children.

"But this model they have been asked to operate under is, quite frankly, madness. It is preset for failure. It is preset for the kids at the top to pretty much succeed on their own, which they would have done anyway, even if not in school. It is preset to teach to the middle, so those in the middle do pretty well, unless there are not enough counselors at the high school level to coach them along until they go on to post-secondary."

"And the kids on the bottom?"

"With this very broken system, sir, most of them don't make it. They drop out of school or stop trying or join a gang or get into some type of dysfunctional lifestyle. And we've known this is the reality for years and years, sir, but we keep coming back every fall and trying it again. That's why I call it madness."

"Well, maybe you're right. But I don't have any more funds to send to your school, Mr. Pearson. With the new football field, the new middle school being built, the community daring us to raise taxes, and state and federal funds diminishing, I just have no choice but to take graciously whatever is given me and then go from there."

"I understand. And, thank you again, sir, for all of these years of important work together. I will always hold you in high regard. Good luck, and have a good life."

REFLECTIONS

1. What dysfunctional processes still exist in your school or district that need to be overhauled or abolished?
2. What successes need to be celebrated?
3. What "new beginnings" would transform your school for its students?

SOLUTIONS

In *Leadership without Easy Answers* (Heifetz, 1994), the uncertainties and perils of this generation are highlighted, indicating that today, perhaps as never before, we thirst for leaders who can effectively navigate organizations toward a better future.

With the current advances in technology and the current alarm across society that the "system" of school has lost ground and is not keeping up with the demands and needs of the twenty-first century, individual schools and their leaders have the capability and need the freedom to invent bold new models for how to best educate their students. Top-down mandates, although well-intended, often cripple the creativity and handcuff the unique needs of local school communities. In the free enterprise system that has made America, removing the compliance definitions of success so more effective school structures and processes can be explored is a huge part of the answer if our schooling system is to even remain relevant in the days ahead.

FIFTEEN

Closing Thoughts

As goes the education of a society, so goes the very fabric of that society.

We live in paradoxical times here in the United States. Our abundance of wealth continues to boggle the mind, yet the poverty and lack of education among our disadvantaged is startling for a nation so steeped in the tradition of being a beacon of hope for the rest of the world.

What are the answers? Politicians, pundits, consultants, and leaders from various other walks of life can't seem to agree. Thus, we find ourselves spinning in what some say is quicksand—an inevitable meltdown that will find "the great society" mired in economic and intellectual ruin in the not-so-distant future.

But, what if?

What if each community was given back its own school, and held accountable to support and love on that school with all of the resources that were available, including human resources?

What if every teacher in every school was given a healthy number of students to work with, a reasonable number, with individual and small group instruction much more the norm (and with instructional assistants, paraprofessionals, and volunteers all part of the process—much like a well-run summer camp)?

What if character education and civic responsibility were the starting point; the foundational piece (not the "add-on" considered as non-essential)?

What if state and federal mandates were much more aggressive in directing funding to communities to develop their schools in fresh and bold new ways?

What if anything that is not in the best interest of age-appropriate education for every student was not allowed in the mix? What would go? What would stay?

What if college students exploring a major in education were immersed in schools as interns from their freshman year? (Thus truly finding out if they are called into the profession, or have less noble reasons to pursue an education degree.)

What if tenure laws were abolished?

What if retirement plans were made more realistic in the twenty-first century, allowing for more individual investment of wages so that burned out or incompetent teachers were allowed to exit the profession swiftly and with dignity (thus also not entrapping very effective teachers who don't feel the need to be in the profession for three decades)?

What if schools were more concerned with meeting the array of needs across the student body, and less concerned with holding on to past traditions which serve mainly the most privileged kids?

What if the most honored and respected profession in our society was that of a teacher?· What if everyone was expected to serve a local school in some way—from high school and college graduates to senior citizens?

What if every school tapped into the technology that is now available for classroom use?

What if every teacher were on a true continuous improvement plan so every year better teaching practices were being mastered?

What if we simply approached the academic success of every student with the fervor and passion that we approach the success of our student athletes?

What if teachers were first and foremost measured by how much they actively cared for the real lives of their students?

What if every teacher did routine home visits, and built trusting relationships with the parents of their students?

What if bullying and harassment in the school culture was so deplored due to the harm it causes beneath the surface that it was non-existent?

What if every school had a rigorous "arts" program, an emphasis on physical fitness, and a robust variety of clubs and enrichment courses on the total menu of student services?

What if education was the core value which every teacher embraced, and was stressed in every classroom as nonnegotiable and more important than power, money, and prestige?

What if the school's "lights were always on" for everyone in the community to have the opportunity to continuously be taking classes of some kind—regardless of age?

Yes, we have come a long way. . . . Yes, we have a long way to go. . . . And, yes, we can dream. And from those dreams wonderful teachers, classrooms, and community schools will emerge. What role do you need to play in helping make your dreams for your community school come true?

REFLECTIONS

1. Does your school spend quality time in truly envisioning the "preferable school of the future"?
2. If so, what are the barriers that prevent your school from reinventing as needed?
3. What needs to take place among staff for this bold vision for the future to be a commonplace conversation in your building?

SOLUTIONS

In *Followership* (Kellerman 2008), the concept of followers taking the lead, as they initiate change while also helping change leaders, opens up new avenues for every organization to be more effective. So, the solutions are already at our fingertips. The missing piece is the increased understanding by more individuals that they (we) must take action, do something, and not accept the status quo. Then the future for your own community school has endless potential to transform and bring holistic health and wellness to your community. One by one, school by school, this "ripple in the pond" approach can indeed transform our society.

References

Babauta, Leo. 2009. *The Power of Less: The Fine Art of Limiting Yourself to the Essential . . . in Business and in Life.* New York: Hyperion.

Child Welfare Information Gateway. www.childwelfare.gov.

Cloud, Henry 2010. *Necessary Endings: The Employees, Businesses, and Relationships that All of Us Have to Give Up in Order to Move Forward.* New York: HarperCollins.

Heifetz, Ronald A. 1994. *Leadership without Easy Answers.* Cambridge, MA: Harvard University Press.

Kellerman, Barbara. 2008. *Followership: How Followers Are Creating Change and Changing Leaders.* Boston: Harvard Business Press.

Kopkowski, Cynthia. 2008. "Why They Leave." *NEA Today Magazine* April 5.

Maslach, Christina, and Michael P. Leiter. 1997. *The Truth about Burnout: How Organizations Cause Personal Stress and What to Do About It.* San Francisco: Jossey-Bass.

Meyerson, Debra E. 2008. *Rocking the Boat: How to Effect Change Without Making Trouble.* Boston: Harvard Business Press.

Miller, Edward, and Joan Almon. 2009. *Crisis In The Kindergarten: Why Children Need to Play in School.* College Park, MD: Alliance for Childhood.

Muhammad, Anthony. 2009. *Transforming School Culture: How to Overcome Staff Division.* Bloomington, IN: Solution Tree Press.

NAEYC Standards for Early Childhood Professional Preparation Programs Position Statement. 2009. http://www.naeyc.org/files/naeyc/file/positions/ProfPrepStandards09.pdf.

National Association for the Education of Young Children. www.naeyc.org.

Palmer, Parker J. 2007. *The Courage to Teach: Exploring the Inner Landscape of a Teacher's Life, 10th edition.* San Francisco, CA: John Wiley & Sons.

Pelzer, Dave. 1995. *A Child Called "It": One Child's Courage to Survive.* London: Orion Publishing Company.

Pink, Daniel H. 2009. *Drive: The Surprising Truth about What Motivates Us.* New York: Penguin.

Raelin, Joseph A. 2003. *Creating Leaderful Organizations: How to Bring Out Leadership in Everyone.* San Francisco: Berrett-Koehler.

Rosales, John. 2011. "Surviving Teacher Burnout." *NEA Today Magazine,* June 7.

Tomlinson, Carol A., Kay Brimijoin, and Lane Narvaez. 2008. *The Differentiated School: Making Revolutionary Changes in Teaching and Learning.* Alexandria, VA: ASCD.

TYC Staff, How to Reduce Stress and Beat Burnout. *Teaching Young Children* 3(1). http://www.naeyc.org/files/tyc/file/How_to_Reduce_Stress_and_Beat_Burnout.pdf.

Williams, Ray. 2011. "Why We Stand by and Don't Help: The Bystander Effect." *Psychology Today,* October 24.

Zemelman, Steven, Harvey Daniels, and Arthur Hyde. 2005. *Best Practice: Today's Standards for Teaching and Learning in America's Shools, 3rd edition.* Portsmouth, NH: Heinemann.

SUGGESTED FURTHER READING

Barnett, David, Carol Christian, Richard Hughes, and Rocky Wallace. 2010. *Privileged Thinking in Today's Schools: The Implications for Social Justice*. Lanham, MD: Rowman & Littlefield Education.

Beaty, Janice J. 2012. *Skills for Preschool Teachers, 9th edition*. Upper Saddle River, NJ: Pearson.

Blanchard, Ken. 1999. *The Heart of a Leader: Insights on the Art of Influence*. Colorado Springs, CO: Honor Books.

Covey, Stephen R. 1992. *Principle-Centered Leadership*. New York: Free Press.

Heifetz, Ronald A., and Martin Linsky. 2002. *Leadership on the Line: Staying Alive through the Dangers of Leading*. Boston: Harvard Business Review Press.

Jensen, Eric. 2009. *Teaching With Poverty in Mind: What Being Poor Does to Kids' Brains and What Schools Can Do About It*. Alexandria, VA: ASCD.

Joiner, William B., and Stephen A. Josephs. 2006. *Leadership Agility: Five Levels of Mastery for Anticipating and Initiating Change*. San Francisco, CA: John Wiley & Sons.

Kouzes, James M., and Barry Z. Posner. 2007. *The Leadership Challenge*. San Francisco, CA: John Wiley & Sons.

Lencioni, Patrick. 2012. *The Advantage: Why Organizational Health Trumps Everything Else*. San Francisco, CA: Jossey-Bass.

Lennick, Doug, and Fred Kiel. 2008. *Moral Intelligence: Enhancing Business Performance and Leadership Success*. Upper Saddle River, NJ: Pearson.

Louv, Richard. 2005. *Last Child in the Woods: Saving Our Children from Nature-Deficit Disorder*. New York: Algonquin Books of Chapel Hill.

Marzano, Robert J. 2007. *The Art and Science of Teaching: A Comprehensive Framework for Effective Instruction*. Alexandria, VA: ASCD.

Murphy, John J. 2010. *Leading With Passion: 10 Essentials for Inspiring Others*. Naperville, IL: Simple Truths, LLC.

Pica, Rae. 2006. *A Running Start: How Play, Physical Activity and Free Time Create A Successful Child*. Cambridge, MA: Da Capo Press: 2006.

Quinn, Robert E. 1996. *Deep Change: Discovering the Leader Within*. San Francisco, CA: Jossey-Bass.

Rath, Tom, and Barry Conchie. 2009. *Strengths Based Leadership: Great Leaders, Teams, and Why People Follow*. New York: Gallup Press.

Serviovanni, Thomas J. 2004. *Strengthening the Heartbeat: Leading and Learning Together in Schools*. San Francisco, CA: Jossey-Bass.

Silver, Harvey F., Richard W. Strong, and Matthew J. Perini. 2000. *So Each May Learn: Integrating Learning Styles and Multiple Intelligences*. Alexandria, VA: ASCD.

About the Authors

Robin Johns has taught in early childhood for twenty-seven years, and is presently a college instructor and the coordinator of the Interdisciplinary Early Childhood Education Program at Ashland Community & Technical College. She has published two children's books and one adult devotional. She is a younger sister to Rocky. She and her husband, Gene, have four children and live on a small farm near Catlettsburg, Kentucky.

Rocky Wallace, EdD, is assistant professor of graduate education and the coordinator of the Principal Licensure Program at Asbury University. He is a former principal of a US Blue Ribbon School, and has authored four previous books on the principalship and servant leadership for Rowman & Littlefield. He and his wife, Denise, have two daughters and live on a small farm near Winchester, Kentucky.